UPROOTING FEAR
How to Flourish Beyond Anxiety and Depression

Amanda Rosen

Rosen House Publishing

LEXINGTON, KY

Copyright © 2023 by **Amanda Rosen**

Unless otherwise indicated, all Scripture quotations are taken from the New King James Version®. Copyright © 1982 by Thomas Nelson. Used by permission. All rights reserved.

Scripture quotations marked (AMP) are taken from the Amplified Bible, Copyright © 2015 by The Lockman Foundation. Used by permission.

Scripture quotations marked (TPT) are from The Passion Translation®. Copyright © 2017, 2018, 2020 by Passion & Fire Ministries, Inc. Used by permission. All rights reserved. ThePassionTranslation.com.

Scripture quotations marked (NLT) are taken from the *Holy Bible*, New Living Translation, copyright © 1996, 2004, 2015 by Tyndale House Foundation. Used by permission of Tyndale House Publishers, Carol Stream, Illinois 60188, USA. All rights reserved.

Scripture quotations marked (NIV) are taken from the Holy Bible, New International Version®, NIV®. Copyright © 1973, 1978, 1984, 2011 by Biblica, Inc.™ Used by permission of Zondervan. All rights reserved worldwide. www.zondervan.com The "NIV" and "New International Version" are trademarks registered in the United States Patent and Trademark Office by Biblica, Inc.™

Scripture quotations marked (MSG) or "The Message" are taken from The Message. Copyright 1993, 1994, 1995, 1996, 2000, 2001, 2002. Used by permission of NavPress Publishing Group. http://www.navpress.com/
Italicized text in Scripture quotations indicates author's emphasis.

Cover by Tayyabah Noor

Library of Congress Cataloging-in-Publication Data is on file at the Library of Congress, Washington, DC.
All rights reserved. No part of this publication may be reproduced, stored in a retrieval system, or transmitted in any form or by any means–electronic, mechanical, digital, photocopy, recording, or any other–except for brief quotations in printed reviews, without prior permission of the publisher.
Printed in the United States of America
Book Layout © 2017 BookDesignTemplates.com

UPROOTING FEAR - How to Flourish Beyond Anxiety and Depression /Amanda Rosen—1st ed.

Copyright © 2023 by Rosen House Books - Lexington, KY

ISBN 978-1-7364973-1-9

Dedication

Dedicated to those who are still waiting for their test to become a testimony.

I leave the gift of peace with you – my peace. Not the kind of fragile peace given by the world, but my perfect peace. Don't yield to fear or be troubled in your hearts – instead, be courageous!

—John 14:27 (TPT)

INTRODUCTION

This book has been almost five years in the making for a couple of reasons. On the positive side, the Lord had me take a break from working on it for about a year to focus elsewhere. As I reflect on that year, I can see that it wasn't just about accomplishing other things; God was adding to my testimony and giving me more to write about. The other reason is not so great. Satan has thrown unbelievable attacks and distractions my way as I got close to completing the book. Once I set my mind on finishing it, Satan set his mind on stopping me. For example, I tried to go away with a friend to her cabin for a few days so I could really focus on finishing the book, but the very first night we were there, the power went out while we were sleeping because a winter storm had rolled in. We never regained power, and I could not write because my laptop had died. That was the beginning of multiple outrageous attacks from the enemy to keep me distracted and discouraged. Even as I'm writing now, our eight-year-old son who was sleeping came into the room to tell me his throat is sore. It has been constant! But you know what? The fact that Satan has fought me so hard to get this book published tells me that somebody out there really needs it and that somebody could be you!

If you're on the outside peeking into my life, it looks pretty great. I'm a stay-at-home mom with four boys that range in age from seven to twenty-three. We've been homeschooling since our oldest was in second grade. I have an amazing husband who has a great job. We live in an expensive part of town, in a huge home, and have terrific neighbors.

For the most part, my life is pretty wonderful, but I didn't get here without trials. The whole reason I am writing this book is because I spent over forty years being bound by fear, anxiety, and depression. When you are dealing with any of those things, you may feel like nothing will ever change, but after decades of battling those demons, I am living proof that you can be set free. My hope is that by taking you on this journey with me, it won't take you as long as it did for me to find freedom.

I'm going to share with you some very dark times in my life; some that I've never spoken about to anyone. I am nervous about sharing certain things that my parents never knew about me. I'm concerned that my children may someday read this book and learn things about me that I just couldn't bring myself to tell them in person. Perhaps it will help them understand that we are all humans who make mistakes and go through trials. No one is exempt, not even their mother.

With my past behind me, I have a new perspective now. I know that sharing my story is a part of my healing and I hope that it will be a part of yours as well. I also pray that as you read the pages in this book, you will feel a new boldness rising up within you to share your own story. **Sometimes the freedom you are seeking can only be found by voicing what you've gone through.** You don't have to write a book or tell the whole world. Just talking to a person or two that you trust can be so freeing. Some of you may have been hurt because you shared your story with the wrong person. The enemy's plan is to use that against you, so you keep walls up and not allow people in. Be prayerful about who to share with. He will lead you to a trustworthy person who will support you on your journey to healing.

God has given me revelations to share with those who are currently walking through the wilderness and for people who have been trying so hard to find freedom from fear, anxiety, and depression, but the struggle still remains. Hearing the testimony of those who have gone through what you are going through is one way to build up your faith. Romans 10:17 says, "So then faith comes by hearing, and hearing by the word of God." I'm here to share the Good News. Christ has set me free, and I know He can do the same for you.

PRAY

Before we go any further, I've written out a prayer to help get you started. It would be best if you would read this part out loud. I pray you feel a shift take place in your life as you read it. Your prayers are powerful!

Father God, I thank You for Your mercy and grace. I thank You that You didn't give up on me, nor will You ever! I pray You will give me divine revelation as I read through this book. I pray that this will be a pivotal moment in my life; a true turning point, away from everything that's held me captive. Lord, I ask You to open my ears to hear from You and to soften my heart to fully receive what You have to say. I pray You will place the right people in my life to come alongside me to help me through this journey.

I ask You, God, for strength to face every fiery dart that the enemy would try to throw my way. Clothe me in the whole armor of God, as in Ephesians chapter six. When I have done all that I know to do, help me stand as You continue fighting for me. Lord, I repent for every time that I have worried instead of trusting You. If there's any part of my life that I need to see in a new light, I pray You will reveal it to me now. Expose it and help me deal with it immediately.

I command every evil spirit to exit right now in the name of Jesus. Right now! Fear, torment, anxiety, panic, depression, oppression, confusion, and every other demonic spirit, GO, in the name of Jesus. You MUST flee at the sound of that name. I command healing in my mind right now!

Lord, I ask You for your supernatural peace to come now and flood my soul. Peace, saturate my soul until it overflows. God, help me to quickly recognize the plans of the enemy even before he tries to attack me and instead of retreating to fear, help me start speaking Your name and commanding peace. I praise You for all that You are about to do in my life. In Jesus's name, Amen.

MY PRAYER OVER YOUR LIFE

I want to expand on that prayer you just prayed by speaking more truth into your life.

You are more than a conqueror through Christ! It doesn't matter what you've been facing. It doesn't matter how messed up your life is or what your past looks like. Today is a new day!

If you've been living in fear or dealing with anxiety, I can promise you that you have a high calling on your life. The warfare has been heavy because Satan sees what you are capable of and he uses fear and anxiety to hold you back. It's the same with depression. Satan knows that if he can keep you in bed, he can keep you from advancing God's kingdom. Do not doubt your position as a son or daughter of the MOST HIGH GOD! He has clothed you in righteousness and has crowned you with a crown of victory. He loves you and desires peace in your life.

I speak to depression right now in the name of Jesus. I bind you! I call out, oh sleeper, arise! The time is now! Get up! Do not continue taking steps backward! Stop going in circles! I command energy to rise up out of the dark places that it's been hiding. I command joy to be restored! I command the joy of the Lord to come and hit you like a mighty rushing wave. The glory that you carry is needed in others' lives. Satan has caused you to miss out on opportunities to pour into others by making you feel unworthy and broken. CHILD OF GOD, YOU ARE NOT UNWORTHY OR BROKEN! The time is NOW to force yourself out of the confinement that the enemy has placed on you. Take the first step and keep putting one foot in front of the other and WATCH HOW THE LORD WILL USE YOU!

I prophesy a transformation in your mind, starting RIGHT NOW! The devil's time is up in Jesus's name! Tormenting thoughts must go! I break the enemy's assignment off your life right now. You shall LIVE and NOT DIE! You are MIGHTY and POWERFUL through Him who created you with a tremendous purpose. I command your mind to be refreshed and to line up with the Word of God, THE WORD OF TRUTH! In Jesus's name! Amen.

CONTENTS

FACING THE PAST 1
THE NEED FOR CONTROL 13
WHERE NEGATIVE SEEDS WERE PLANTED 23
ANXIETY AND OBEDIENCE 33
THE ROOT OF ALL FEARS 45
A LIFE RUINED WITH REGRET 53
WISDOM OR FEAR? 63
DEPRESSION 73
FROM FEAR TO VICTORY 91
WHAT FREEDOM LOOKS LIKE 105
THE KEYS TO HEALING AND DELIVERANCE 117
ACKNOWLEDGEMENTS 137

CHAPTER ONE

FACING THE PAST

From before I was even born, Satan plotted how he could destroy my life. He has the same plan for you!

I Peter 5:8 says, "Be sober, be vigilant; because your adversary the devil walks about like a roaring lion, seeking whom he may devour." If you feel you can't catch a break, it's because God has a great purpose for your life. The Lord knows what you are capable of. You are a deliverer! Satan has always wanted to kill deliverers, so be watchful at all times and don't fall prey to his lies. Also, know you are not going through hard times in vain. The reason for the pain is that one day you will help others walk through dark valleys into a place of freedom. The pain is a part of the preparation process to equip you to go where God is calling you. II Corinthians 1:3-4 says,

Blessed be the God and Father of our Lord Jesus Christ, the Father of mercies and God of all comfort, who comforts us in all our tribulation, that we may be able to comfort those who are in any trouble, with the comfort with which we ourselves are comforted by God.

Do you know what fear really is? Fear is believing the enemy's lies. God doesn't plant fear in your mind; only Satan does.

When you feel fear taking over, it's because something Satan has told you has become greater than the truth of God's Word.

The more time you spend with God, the easier it will be to separate God's truth from the enemy's lies. Put your faith in God instead of living in fear and stop believing everything the devil whispers in your ear.

My mother had two sons and had longed to have a daughter. In her despair, she went to her grandmother, who was nearing the end of life on earth, and told her to ask Jesus to send her a baby girl. My mom knows we can talk directly to Jesus, and He hears us, but her heart was yearning for a baby girl. Sometimes we do strange things when we're desperate, but I believe those desperate moments of sheer determination are when faith arises and breakthrough begins.

When my brother Davie was about six years old, my mom started bleeding unexpectedly. She bled for six whole weeks before she finally went to get it checked out. Imagine her surprise and the fear she must have felt when the doctor told her she was pregnant! I believe this was Satan's first attempt to take me out. Perhaps he knew I would grow up loving the Lord. But guess what? Satan can't destroy what God has ordained!

If you're reading this right now, then you better believe God created you for a great purpose. I'm sure you've already overcome a lot of adversity. God never told us it would be easy, but He did promise He would never leave us or forsake us. If it seems like God is nowhere to be found, then ask yourself if you're the one who has gone astray. If you've been seeking the Lord with all your heart, then rest assured, He has heard every prayer and will work things out for His glory if you continue to trust Him.

For my mom, her heart's desire to have a little girl of her own became a reality when she found out she was pregnant with me.

When I picture her carrying me in her stomach, I envision Jesus holding me in her womb, protecting me from Satan's destruction.

For You formed my inward parts; You covered me in my mother's womb. Psalm 139:13

When my mom was pregnant with me, she had a tear in her uterus that had to be cauterized. They put her on bed rest for so long that she ended up pulling my brother out of kindergarten because she couldn't walk him up the hill to catch the school bus. My brother remembers this differently, but this is the story my mom always told me, so I'm sticking with it. My mom faced three months of uncertainty and fear of what would happen to the baby growing inside her. Several months after my mom was put on bed rest, God's glory prevailed, and she was able to make it to full term and deliver me with no issues. I was her first child she got to deliver while she was awake. Can you believe it used to be routine to put women to sleep during labor? If that's not true, then my mom lied to me.

I don't have too many memories of myself as a young child. I know I always spent more time with adults than with kids my age and I loved holding all the babies in my family every chance I could get. Beyond that, the earliest memories I can recall involve a man I love with all my heart, and I would never want to hurt him. He's someone who has taught me about hard work, sacrifice, and never giving up. He will do anything for anyone. Today, I have nothing but love and respect for him, but it hasn't always been this way. This man I'm talking about is my dad.

Some of my earliest memories as a child are with him. When he was sober, he was my world. I'll never forget going to an island on Lake Erie every year for vacation. It wasn't Disney World, but it was perfect for our family. We would go fishing, explore caves, ride golf carts all around town, eat a lot of yummy junk food, visit nature centers, and do a ton of shopping where my parents would buy me new dog figurines to add to my ever-growing collection. Some years we camped in tents and other times we rented cottages. I remember riding bicycles around the campsites, playing at the local playground, and going swimming in the lake. Some years it was just the five of us and other years we brought extra family or friends along with us. Spending those summers with my cousins and my best friends were some of the most memorable times of my life.

More awesome childhood memories took place at the farm where I grew up. My big, light-green farmhouse at the end of a long, private lane still sits in my mind as clear as day. Green probably sounds so ugly for a house, but I never thought it was. It was a place full of great adventure and I was a free spirit who loved to explore! Some of my fondest memories there revolved around caring for our animals. It was the best chore ever, for me at least. I never had to do the hard and stinky work like my brothers. They had to shovel cow poop out of the barn. Yuck! One of my favorite pastimes was feeding my baby calves with a bottle. It was a super messy chore that I absolutely loved.

It's crazy how I can remember things in such great detail all these years later. I can still hear the black baby calf with a white lightning bolt design on its forehead, slurping up the milk as it dripped down from the huge, white bottle it was tugging on. Oh, how I loved that sweet baby! The strong smell of hay after a cold and rainy day drowned out most of the other smells. I can also smell the wet animals in the barn and the strong manure scent that never went away, no matter how clean the barn was. Those smells never bothered me back then because you get used to stuff like that after a while. Now, whenever I catch a whiff of wet barn animals, it brings me right back to the place I called home so many years ago.

We had cows that were so gentle we could ride them, ducks that came up to our front door for me to pet and love on, and all sorts of dogs, cats, pigs, chickens, and roosters. Sometimes I wish I could go back to that way of living, but then I think about all the work it takes to run a farm. On top of all the animal work and keeping up with the property and yard, we also had an enormous garden each year. We planted all kinds of produce. The garden was a daily, sweaty task each of us worked on. As my dad hoed each row, I **would** go along behind him, dropping seeds into their place. As we were waiting for the crops to appear, we had to keep the garden watered and continuously pull weeds so they wouldn't overtake the plants.

Once the harvest was ready, I helped pick the fruits and vegetables and Dad would dig up the ones that were buried underground. I have memories of snapping green beans and removing the strings with my mom and Grandma to prepare them to be canned. It seemed like there was a never-ending supply of beans! My hands would become sore from snapping so many beans and it looked like the big bucket of unsnapped beans wasn't getting any smaller. We weren't just snapping beans though; we were making memories that would last a lifetime as I listened to my grandma talk about all the important things in life like God, church, and family. Those moments of hard work are now some of my most cherished memories.

For fun on the farm, I'd ride my bike up and down our long driveway. I couldn't see any neighbors, just fields, cows, and tall corn stalks. When I wasn't riding my bike, you could find me on the lawn mower driving around aimlessly for hours. I was so scrawny my dad had to put concrete blocks under my seat to weigh it down enough for me to ride, otherwise, it wouldn't even start. I also have fond memories of singing karaoke in my bedroom until my parents made me go to bed, catching snakes in the yard (so hard to believe now), and climbing trees. I was quite the tomboy. I guess that came easily with two older brothers!

Dad took me fishing a lot. Many of our best memories were made on a lake or next to a pond somewhere. Sometimes I joke about fish being his first true love. I feel like there are more pictures of him holding up a crappie or a largemouth bass than there are pictures of the two of us together. When I was about twelve years old, we were fishing in a huge pond somewhere. I yelled for my dad to get the net because I hooked a big one! He ran over and took my pole, and at first, he thought my line was snagged. I kept telling him I knew there was a fish on it. Sure enough, it was the biggest catfish I'd ever seen in my life. Dad was so proud of me. I'll never forget his excitement in that moment. Nothing makes his eyes light up more than a large fish stuck to the end of a fishing line that belongs to him or someone he cares about.

We also went to a lot of car shows. I always had to get my picture taken next to every red convertible we came across. I don't know why, but that was my favorite car. It didn't matter what make, model, or year it was; I loved all red convertibles! Dad also took me to a lot of flea markets where I felt like his little princess. He'd buy me almost anything I asked for. Now that I'm all grown up, I realize just how cheap all those things were, but I'm still glad he rarely said no to me.

I'm so thankful for all the sweet memories I had with my dad because it wasn't always like that. There's a painful side that's hard to talk about: the part where he was an abusive alcoholic.

MY EARLIEST DARK MEMORIES

I had to pause when I got to this point because I was unable to continue writing for several weeks. Sometimes when you bring up the past, it causes you to relive it. The pain comes back, and you can feel it just as if you are right back there where it all happened. I had so many amazing memories as a little girl, but then there was a dark side too; the part that wishes to stay buried. But I'm pulling it all back to the surface to let you know you are not alone and to encourage you to keep walking toward the light.

And the light shines in the darkness, and the darkness did not comprehend it.
John 1:5

I picture myself on the bed in my small bedroom at the farm, hiding in the darkness. There was no door on my room, which was just on the other side of the living room. One step down from the living room led to our dining room and kitchen, where all the chaos was unfolding. I can hear the fury from my dad as he screamed at my mother. Even though I can't physically see my dad's face from where I was hiding, I knew it was beet red because that's how it always looked during his raging fits. I hear my mom standing up for herself and giving Dad a taste of his own medicine. I hear such foul things being said. Words that can't be taken back. Words that would scar my innocent soul for years to come.

I remember one argument my parents had. Again, I was hiding in my bedroom. I think they thought I was asleep, but it was impossible to sleep through all the noise. It escalated so badly that my mom got a gun from wherever they kept them hidden. Suddenly, my dad's demeanor changed, and he started apologizing to my mom. He thought she was about to commit suicide right there in front of him. He was begging her not to do it. That's when my mother said she wasn't going to kill herself; she was going to shoot him. She finally had enough of all the abuse. I stayed hidden in my room, crying and praying no one would get hurt.

It was difficult as a little girl to watch my daddy behave the way he did when he was consumed with alcohol. It was even tougher to watch out the window on that dark and rainy night as they took him away in handcuffs and put him into the police car. The red and blue lights were glaring as my dad sat in the backseat with his head hung low. Once his door was shut, all I could see was his shadow as the rain beat down on his window, forming giant beads of water that would race down the foggy glass. I'm guessing I was probably around nine years old. Though scared and confused and extremely sad he was gone; I was relieved my home was finally peaceful and everyone was safe.

At least a year had passed since the night Dad was taken to jail and my mom finally got up the nerve to leave him. We moved in with my Mamaw and my mother filed for a divorce. That season of my life is etched in my mind forever. My Mamaw's house differed greatly from the farm I was used to. It was a two-story home with blue concrete block walls. We had the entire second floor to ourselves and Mamaw lived on the first floor, but we were free to go up and down as we pleased. There was a small yard in front of the house, lined with the biggest, most beautiful rose bushes I'd ever seen. To the right of the house was a long driveway and then a bigger yard that was mostly fenced in. My favorite part of the yard was an enormous willow tree that just seemed magical to me. It was ginormous! I can still picture myself as a little girl, staring up at all the beautiful branches that seemed to dance gently with even the slightest breeze. I often lost track of time playing under that marvelous, mesmerizing tree. Did you know as raindrops fall to the ground from the drooping branches of the willow tree, it resembles tears? That's where the name weeping willow comes from. And now I find myself weeping as I bring to the surface the memories that I would rather forget.

My Mamaw was a Pentecostal preacher, so we often went with her to church on Sundays. Her church was on Marshall Avenue in downtown Cincinnati. Experiencing the streets of Cincinnati was like stepping into a completely new world to me. I always noticed half-dressed people hanging out by the streets of my Mamaw's church, but my innocent mind thought nothing of it. Now I understand why my mom always clenched my hand as she walked with me through the front door. No matter how loud the service would get, those doors remained open the entire time. Can you imagine that happening today? Now churches have to keep their doors shut and have armed guards waiting nearby.

I know my Mamaw helped save the souls of many lost people; some who just wandered into the church to escape the elements outside and others who needed a place to rest their weary heads. What a bold lady my grandmother was! I imagine most people wouldn't have the courage to hold church services in such a place, let alone keep the doors open.

My mother told me a story about a woman who always stood outside of my Mamaw's church, afraid to come in because she couldn't afford clothes that looked nice. My mom said this lady always wore clothes that seemed like they were too small for her. The way my mom told the story, I picture someone who may have had a drug addiction or other struggles in life. Mamaw insisted she should come in for service, regardless of her appearance or lifestyle. She told the lady that it was her job to get her through the doors and God's job to clean her up. And that's exactly what happened!

While living with Mamaw, I got to spend a lot of time with my cousins, which helped take my mind off what was going on with my parents. For about a year, my dad would try to come around occasionally to spend time with me. I dreaded my visitations with him. Every single time, he'd take me places to buy stuff. There was a point in my life when I loved going shopping with him, but this time was different. I felt like he didn't know how to interact with me, and he was just trying to buy my love. I wanted my mom and dad to get back together so badly. I missed being a family. I missed my animals, my old friends, and my life as I once knew it. Every night before I closed my eyes, I prayed for a miracle.

I know God heard my prayers! Before the divorce became final, my dad stopped drinking and my parents ended up getting back together. It was a long road for the whole family. It took a lot of AA meetings and counseling for all of us to find the healing and recovery that we needed. There were still plenty of arguments in our home, but without alcohol in the picture, they weren't as terrible. This year my parents celebrated fifty-three years of marriage! Their story reminds me of that old willow tree. Though many storms blew through and tried to tear it down, it stood strong through the years.

REFLECT

I wrote about my childhood because I've learned that reliving the parts of your past that you usually try not to think about can give you answers and help you move on and let go.

Facing your past instead of ignoring it is sometimes necessary to find true freedom.

What is it you need to face today? What is that thing that's buried deep inside of you? Maybe no one else even knows about it, but you secretly think about it almost every single day. Or maybe you almost completely forgot about it because you'd rather pretend it never happened, instead of confronting it. I know how much it hurts to dig up what has been buried, but I encourage you to press in and don't just toss this book to the side and forget about it. This is a key step toward true freedom. How bad do you want to be free?

At the end of each chapter, I've included a separate page "My Reflections Page" for you to write down your thoughts. In the next chapter we will continue pressing toward real freedom by reliving those dark moments that are so hard to face.

My Reflections

CHAPTER TWO

THE NEED FOR CONTROL

On October 17, 2018, I went to a friend's house so she and another friend could pray for me. Fear had such a tight grip on my life, and I needed healing from an issue I was having with my throat. It turned out to be something minor, but I had convinced myself that it was something terrible, like esophageal cancer. Little did I know that my childhood would be brought up at my friend's house because we were trying to get to the root of my fear. So here I was again, reliving those terrifying moments as a little girl. I don't remember my dad ever physically doing anything more than spanking me, but the verbal abuse was bad enough. They say sticks and stones can break your bones, but words can never hurt you. I don't know where that saying came from because, for me, the pain of my dad's words damaged my soul for many years. Although I don't remember him ever laying a hand on me, I do remember plenty of fights between my dad and my older brothers. They would be out in the front yard throwing punches at each other while my mother screamed at them to stop. It was a frightful sight to see.

During the prayer meeting with my friends, one of them asked me, "Where was Jesus when this was going on? Can you picture Him?" Wow! I had never thought about that before. But as I sat there with my eyes closed, taking my mind back to focus on those horrible memories, I saw the Lord holding me and wiping away my tears as I hid in my room. I also saw Him protecting my mom and my brothers from tragedy. He kept my mom from pulling the trigger the night that she was about to murder my dad. One firing of that gun would have drastically changed the course of all our lives, but Jesus stopped it from happening.

My friend took me back to several other memories, and it was in those flashbacks that I saw that my deeply rooted fears had caused me to become a control freak. We are not born with a desire to be in control. As infants, we rely completely on other humans. The need for control is learned through life experiences. It usually comes through situations that cause you to lose trust in those you once relied on. I needed to be in control of most areas of my life, but I never even thought it was an issue until I realized it was driven by fear. **Do you realize that the need for control equals a lack of trust in God?** I didn't trust God with much of my life.

Since the time I got married at twenty-seven, I wouldn't let my husband Aaron drive the car; I always had to be the one in the driver's seat. I've also been afraid to fly in an airplane because then I would have zero control. This need for control had ruined my life, and I have missed out on so much of the Lord's great creation. By being in the driver's seat, I've missed out on some amazing scenery. There have been many times when my kids would say, "Whoa, look at that!" but I couldn't because I had to focus on the road. And because of my fear of flying, I missed out on an all-inclusive trip to Mexico with my husband. In a later chapter, I'll tell you more about this trip and how it was a pivotal turning point in my life.

As my friends and I continued to delve deeper into my past, we learned that the moment my oldest son Gavin was born is when my need for control completely took over my life. It was my job to protect that baby and raise him the right way. I wasn't going to let anything bad happen to him. Again, my friend asked, "Can you see Jesus there at the birth of your first son?"

I paused for just a few seconds and then tears began to roll down my face. *I vividly saw Jesus. He wasn't just in the room with me. He is the one who caught my son as he came out of the womb.* God not only formed Gavin in my womb, but He was there to catch him at birth, and He's been there every second of every day since then.

This encounter with my friends happened about four years ago, but as I was writing this book, the Lord showed me something incredible one morning during my usual Bible study time. I was reading through a plan on the Bible app when the words from Isaiah 46:3 jumped out at me and completely took me by surprise. The words immediately took me back to the moment my first son was born, and it solidified my faith in what I saw as I envisioned his birth. The Amplified version says, "Listen to Me," [says the LORD], "O house of Jacob, and all the remnant of the house of Israel, **You who have been carried by Me from your birth and have been carried [in My arms] from the womb.**"

God is so amazing that He didn't stop there! He gave me THREE more verses just to further prove His involvement in my son's birth.

Lord, you delivered me safely from my mother's womb. You are the one who cared for me ever since I was a baby. Psalm 22:9 TPT

It continues in Psalm 22:10, "Since the day I was born, I've been placed in your custody. You've cradled me throughout my days, and you've always been my God."

By You I have been upheld from birth; You are He who took me out of my mother's womb. My praise shall be continually of You. Psalm 71:6

Isn't that just mind-blowing? Can you picture that? He was there for your birth. Since you're reading this, then it means that you were born, and you can stand on the fact that He was the one who delivered you and He has been caring for you ever since!

The Lord just dropped something into my spirit that I need to address before I continue. I see women reading this book who have suffered the loss of a child. It may upset you at first because the enemy will try to lie to you and make you think God wasn't there to deliver your baby. First, I want to say that I'm incredibly sorry for what you have endured. I can't imagine how hard that must have been. Truly, my heart breaks for you even though I don't know you. Second, I can assure you that God was there. He received your child into His loving arms and has cared for that sweet baby ever since, just like His Word says. That was for your baby too!

May I prophesy over your life for just a second? This is for anyone grieving the loss of a loved one. The Lord is a Lord who restores. He will restore your broken heart and trade your ashes for beauty. You WILL heal from that experience and your healing will be used for His glory. You will be a light in the life of someone else who has to walk that same path. Joy will return and you will not spend every day in grief. There is a season for the grief, but it is not God's desire for you to hold on to the pain and sorrow forever. Release it ALL to Him and watch what He will do.

Ask the Lord to show you exactly what you are holding on to. (Now I'm talking to everyone again, not just those who have experienced the loss of someone close.) Sometimes we think we've given all our junk to God, but when we get really honest with Him, He'll show us another area that still has a hold on our lives. He may reveal something that you've never even considered before if you just let Him know you are truly ready to hand it all over to Him. Is it bitterness? Jealousy? Anger? Hurt? The attention that you get by holding on to the pain? Something else? He's waiting for you to lay every bit down at His feet so He can start working in your life in ways that you can't even imagine.

When my friends helped me see where the Lord was during those critical moments in my own life, it was like I took a huge leap forward toward the freedom that God always intended for me to walk in. I know now that whenever I face trials, even if I can't see Him, He's there. He's always been there for you too. ALWAYS! He has a purpose for everything we go through.

There may have been moments in your life where you were angry with Him because you were certain that God wouldn't allow such a horrible thing to happen. Maybe that's the moment where you started believing that you needed to be in control because you thought you couldn't trust God anymore.

One day I was talking to a friend who has overcome so much adversity in her life. She's gone through things that I find hard to even imagine, like homelessness and extremely abusive relationships. While I was talking to her, I had a vision. You may have heard the story of the donkey that fell in a hole and tried to get out. Well, I pictured that story, but only with my friend instead of a donkey. I saw her way down deep in the bottom of a dark and dirty pit, getting bombarded with the heavy weight of dirt being shoveled on top of her by people up at the top. Do you feel like that? Do you feel knocked down by the weight of the world, finding it so hard to just move forward in life? Does it seem like everyone is looking down on you and that perhaps you've been forgotten about or left behind? Does your past leave you feeling dirty and unworthy?

Well, guess what I saw next? As the people kept throwing dirt down into the pit, little did they know that every time they piled the dirt on her, she would shake it off and use it to take a step up. It's hard to see when you're in the pit. Everything around you just seems so dirty and dark. It's difficult to have hope when you can't imagine any way out. But don't give up because soon enough you will find yourself at the top, where no one will be able to try to bury you in the dirt again. Sure, life may still throw some dust your way, but it won't be enough to weigh you down. Keep persevering!

Don't be like the Israelites! Even after all the miracles God had performed for them, they still questioned whether the Lord was among them or not. This was during their walk in the wilderness. Are you in the wilderness right now? Or maybe it feels more like a dark cave. Are you feeling hopeless and doubting that God even exists? The Israelites had already witnessed the plagues, the parting of the Red Sea, bread from heaven, and quail every day, but they were so thirsty that they started doubting again. (See Exodus 17:7)

What miracles have you seen in your life? Think about that for a minute. No really! Pause right here and think back to last year, ten years ago, or maybe go all the way back to your childhood.

You may have witnessed some crazy miracles in your life. Personally, I've experienced several healings in my body, been spared from many near tragic accidents, and God has given us provision time after time when we were about to go under financially. Don't forget what the Lord has already done for you! You may not think much of it, but you're alive and breathing and that alone is a miracle! Since there is still breath in your lungs, it's not too late for the Lord to prove Himself faithful in your life. Philippians 1:6 says, "being confident of this very thing, that He who has begun a good work in you will complete *it* until the day of Jesus Christ". That means that He is faithful to finish what He started, but it will most likely require work on your end. Your next step forward could be the very step necessary to break the current cycle you've been stuck in and propel you into the future that God has prepared for you.

REFLECT

This may be one of the most difficult things you've done in quite some time. You need to allow your mind to take you back to that moment when fear had a tight grip around your neck. Or to the moment when someone hurt you. Or the time you messed up. Perhaps it's the day your life significantly changed in a great way, like the day my first son was born. Use your notes from the previous chapter if you're having trouble figuring out where to start.

*Whatever memory comes to your mind,
it's time to see things differently!*

Pause right here and find a quiet place where you can think in peace for a few. I've included a place for you to write down anything that Holy Spirit brings to your mind.

- Close your eyes and ask the Lord to show you where He was in that situation.
- Get lost in the moment as you search for God. If it doesn't come to you right away, don't get discouraged. Ask Holy Spirit to help you see Jesus.
- Focus on that memory until you see Him. He was there! He has always been there.
- Now think about the things that cause fear in your life.

Does it make you feel better if you try to control the situations surrounding your fears? If so, do you think that control really does anything good for you? Sometimes I wonder if God laughs at us. We think we have so much control over certain things, but really, we can do nothing apart from Him. The day that you scoot on over to the passenger seat in life and let God take the wheel, I promise you that things will change in your life. You may have to do it afraid for a while, but as you push through those fears, you'll discover all the blessings that you've been missing out on.

My Reflections

CHAPTER THREE

WHERE NEGATIVE SEEDS WERE PLANTED

When I was twelve years old, I started having stabbing pains in the middle of my chest. The discomfort was so intense that it brought me to tears. My crying persuaded my parents to take me to the emergency room more than once. The first time, I had several tests done but everything came back normal, and they sent me home on pain medication. Then during another trip to the ER, a doctor took a simple chest x-ray which revealed the issue. I had a pea-sized tumor in the middle of my breastbone. The good news (which I'm not sure how they could tell without a biopsy or any further tests) was that it was benign. In case you're like me and have to look this word up, I'll save you the effort. It means not cancerous.

After some consultations with a specialist, my parents decided it would be best if I had surgery to remove the tumor. Because my family was so concerned about the outcome of the procedure, they planned a huge party for my thirteenth birthday which was right around the corner. I had a blast playing with all my cousins and friends, opening so many thoughtful gifts, and blowing out the candles on my Bart Simpson birthday cake. It made me feel so loved to see how many people came to share my special day with me.

Late that night, long after the party was over, I sat my little exhausted body down in our orangish-red and brown, plaid rocking chair. I leaned back to get comfy when suddenly, I felt a horrible sting on my spine in the dead center of my back. Growing up on a farm I had gotten stung many times, so at first, this had little effect on me. But I learned quickly that this time wouldn't be like all the others.

Just minutes after the wasp had stung me, my eyes felt like they were on fire. When I told my mom that my eyes were burning badly, she looked at me in a state of panic. What I didn't realize was that my eyes were swelling shut! My dad had gone to a little store in town to buy some baking soda to help with the sting site and this was back before everybody had cell phones, so he did not know what was unfolding at home. Just minutes after my eyes began to swell shut, I started breaking out with hives all over my body and my legs shook fiercely and uncontrollably. My heart felt like it was going to explode because it was pounding so hard. As soon as my mother realized that I was going into anaphylactic shock, she called 911. The operator told her to wrap a cold, wet towel around my neck to help prevent my airways from closing and they stayed on the phone with her until the ambulance showed up.

Boy was my dad in for a surprise when he got home from the store and saw an ambulance in the driveway! Since we lived out in the country, it was about a half-hour drive to the nearest hospital. The ride there was one I'll never forget. It was dark out and I was so scared. Sirens blared all the way to the hospital, and I could tell we were moving fast. The speed we were traveling made me more anxious because it made me realize the seriousness of the situation. The paramedics tried several times to get an IV in my arm, even while racing down a bumpy road that was under construction. I cried as they continued tormenting me over and over with the needle. As if my body wasn't going through enough, now I had to deal with the constant stabs on my hands and arms. It felt like they were lighting a match on my skin each time they touched me. They gave up and waited until we got to the hospital to place the IV. Thank God! Once we were there, I don't know what all they gave me, but I remember feeling very loopy, but finally relaxed. They also put a warm blanket on my body to help me stop shaking. Through it all, my dad didn't seem too concerned until one doctor pulled him aside and told him that this could be fatal. I guess he didn't realize that wasp stings could kill people and that just because my body was relaxed, I still wasn't in the clear.

I'm so grateful that I survived that terrible experience, but this was just one of the events that caused me to start living life differently than I did before. It was one of many seeds of fear that would be planted in me, and because I didn't know any better, they began to grow and develop roots. I abruptly went from being a carefree little girl to living a very restricted and boring life. I no longer ran barefoot outside, feeling the lush grass on my feet. The days of laying out in the sunshine with lemon juice in my hair, without a care in the world, had come to a swift halt. Now every time I tried to relax; I'd hear bees buzzing nearby. It's like I suddenly became super sensitive to a sound that I never seemed to notice before. When a bee or wasp came anywhere near me, I lost all control. Fear and panic took over. Even though I knew the best thing I could do would be to remain still and calm, I would do the exact opposite and run away screaming. After each encounter, my heart would palpitate, and I found it hard to breathe normally. I spent so many days sitting inside my house, crying because I couldn't enjoy being outdoors like I used to. It seemed so unfair. The joy of swimming, hiking, biking, climbing trees, picking berries, riding my lawn mower, and playing with my farm animals are just a few things I felt robbed of because of my newfound fear.

Finishing my thirteenth birthday in the hospital seemed to be a prelude to what was to come. During that year alone, I faced the possibility of major surgery to remove a tumor, I broke my arm, and

I had the first of many surgeries on my ovaries. If you're wondering what happened with the tumor in my chest, what I'm about to tell you might just blow your mind.

It was the morning of the surgery. The surgeon would have to cut my breastbone open (which is directly in front of the heart) to remove the tumor, so this was not a minor surgery by any means. As we were walking out the door of our farmhouse on a crisp summer morning, the phone rang. It was the surgeon himself! You know it's serious when the main person in charge calls. He told my dad that he just couldn't bring himself to go through with the operation because he had never performed that particular surgery on anyone as young as me before. Can you believe that? Sure would've been nice to know that sooner! But I praise the Lord for stopping the plans that the enemy had for me.

When my parents took me to a different specialist, they said that something else had to be causing the level of pain I was experiencing because the tumor was so small. At just thirteen years old, I didn't care what the doctors said. I believed that God was going to heal me! Back then, I went to every church service that I could attend, and most of the time my grandma Peg was the one who took me because my parents were so busy. One night she took me to a revival service somewhere. Those were way cooler to me than normal church services because there was always so much more action, and even though I didn't recognize what it really was back then, now I know it was the power of the Holy Spirit that always got my attention. On this one particular night, the preacher called me out of the crowd and said that there was something in my chest that wasn't supposed to be there. I knew he had heard from the Lord because we didn't know this man and he had no way of knowing that they had diagnosed me with a tumor in my chest.

As I stood there next to Grandma, surrounded by a bunch of people who had gathered around me to pray, I remember the dark-haired, older preacher, laying his hands on me and commanding healing to come. Grandma had one arm around me and held me close to her as the booming echoes of prayer filled the room. Then I looked up and saw tears flowing down her face as she thanked Jesus. I can't fully explain how I was feeling, but it was like a supernatural high. I experienced the presence of God like never before and I knew He had touched my body and I was healed. From that moment on, I never experienced that type of chest pain again!

Many years later, just out of curiosity (fear), I had an x-ray on my chest. It confirmed what my spirit knew; there was no tumor. I recently had another x-ray on my chest because of an odd feeling that I'd been having, and that x-ray was also perfect. Praise the Lord!

It wasn't long after I finally had relief in my chest, that I began experiencing another issue. My side started hurting so bad during my monthly cycles I would be doubled over in paralyzing pain. They soon discovered that I had a cyst on my ovary. The doctors tried treating it with medication, but it just wouldn't go away. Before I knew it, I was in the hospital having my first surgery to remove the cyst. I was still just thirteen years old. Just a couple of years later I found myself back in the hospital having an operation on my other ovary for the same reason. Then at sixteen years old, I had yet another surgery for the same problem. By this point, I felt like a surgery pro. I had gone through it twice, so I didn't expect the third time to be very different; however, when I woke up in the recovery room, the surgeon rambled on about how they had to reconstruct my ovary and how the endometriosis was all over my insides. Then he explained that there was nothing they could do about it because it was newly formed, and it would be like plucking tiny hairs.

Wait! What? Endometriosis? Somehow, I had heard about that, but I wasn't completely sure what it was. The doctor mistakenly thought that my parents had already gone over all the details of the procedure with me, but they hadn't told me anything yet. I think they had gone downstairs to the cafeteria to get a bite to eat while I was still sleeping. The doctor also checked my incision site, and that's when I learned it wasn't just a few small incisions like the previous surgeries. They had cut me open from one side of my stomach to the other. When my parents came back to my room, I was all alone, crying my eyes out. They were very surprised and then angered to know that the doctor had given me the full report. I had already been told that I may never have children, so this new diagnosis left me completely numb. My number one goal in life was to become a mother someday. As I sat there in the hospital bed, I felt more than just physical scars and pain. Although I was only sixteen, the emotional pain felt too heavy to bear.

As I look back on all the medical issues I've endured over my lifetime, I can now see the good and the bad. The good news is that God was truly with me, and He saw me through each trial and now I can help others who face similar situations. Remembering the hard times reminds me of how God brought me through those circumstances every time. He may have not done it the way I had hoped or as quickly as I wanted Him to, but He did it. Now every time I face something that seems impossible, I remember all that God has done for me and remind myself that He can do it again! I never want to forget all that the Lord has done for me.

Let all that I am praise the LORD; may I never forget the good things he does for me. Psalm 103:2 (NLT)

There is a flip side though. As I think about all the medical problems I've had, I can see where each issue was an opportunity for Satan to sow seeds of fear, doubt, depression, and anxiety in my mind. The severe allergic reaction to bees opened the door to all those things. I became so fearful of living a normal life. The fear turned into anxiety and panic. I doubted that my life could ever look how it used to. Then I became depressed as I watched everyone else around me living what seemed to be a normal, happy life, while I felt like a prisoner to the indoors.

The tumor in my breastbone had me questioning whether I could live a long life. Doubt had settled in hard! What if it was cancerous? What if it came back? How would I know? Infertility issues caused me to doubt whether I'd ever be able to carry children in my womb. It caused me to rush wanting to have children, fearful that if I waited too long, my chances of getting pregnant would continue to decrease.

Every new diagnosis showed God and Satan where I stood in my faith.

And if I was fearful or doubtful for even a second, not only did I open a door, but I gave Satan room to put his foot in it. Over the years, Satan learned how to take all my worries and magnify them until I got to where I thought I was going to die if my left arm started hurting or I got a severe headache. When he finds a weak spot, he will be sure to use that to his full advantage.

When even the tiniest negative seed is planted, Satan will cause it to begin to grow and take root in your life if you don't destroy it immediately. You may ask, what is a negative seed? It is any word or action that doesn't line up with the Word of God. I don't include thoughts because there is no scripture that says Satan can hear your thoughts! So be very careful what comes out of your mouth. In chapter five I tell you exactly how to handle negative seeds that have been planted in your life. You don't just accept them and try to move on because plants can still grow when they're being ignored if they're in the right environment.

Negative seeds don't just stem from medical issues as I've discussed so far. There was something that happened in a relationship that I discuss in chapter eight. It was there that seeds of doubt, anxiety, and depression were planted. In an instant, my life changed, and I stopped caring so much about myself. I started seeing myself differently than ever before. I felt shame, guilt, and condemnation. Those seeds grew year after year as I allowed the impact of one boy's actions to keep me from seeing myself the way God sees me. When that experience was coupled with growing up with an alcoholic father, I began to think that there were no good men in the world.

Every negative experience in life is an opportunity for bad seeds to be sown. I have been abused and cheated on, betrayed by friends, witnessed deadly storms, failed at many personal and professional goals, and lost some people who meant the world to me. When you face these situations, it's up to you to recognize that you have a choice. You can allow circumstances to get you down and frustrate you and you can let anger fester so long that it turns into pure hatred. You can dwell on bad thoughts so long that they spiral out of control, and you start believing that nothing good can come from what you've been through. *Or* you can combat defeat by deciding quickly to let go of any offenses, choose forgiveness, and use the authority that God gave you to speak to the mountains in your life.

REFLECT

Is there an area of your life that you would consider a trigger for anxiety, fear, or depression? If you can think back to when that first became an issue in your life, you will see when the negative seeds were planted and when Satan stuck his foot through that door. All is not lost and hopeless, no matter how long you've felt this way. Healing is possible! It doesn't matter how long it's been since you experienced trauma. Although seeds may have grown into the tallest tree in the world, the Lord can pull it out of the ground by the roots in an instant. There are many instances in the Bible where Jesus healed people instantly or within the very hour that He prayed for them. In Hebrews 13:8, we are told that Jesus Christ is the same yesterday, today, and forever. Knowing that, I can reassure you that what He did when He walked the face of this earth in the flesh, He can do for you now, wherever you are reading this book. Don't give up! Write down anything that is important for you to remember from this reflection time.

My Reflections

CHAPTER FOUR

ANXIETY AND OBEDIENCE

For years I would ask God to get rid of my fears. I would recite my favorite Bible verse, II Timothy 1:7, over and over. It says, "God has not given us a spirit of fear, but of power, and of love, and of a sound mind." I always focused on the part that says that He didn't give us a spirit of fear, but one day the Lord had me take another look at that verse.

About ten years ago something crazy began happening during my sleep. I would fall asleep peacefully but then be jolted awake in the middle of the night with my heart racing and my body shaking uncontrollably. It reminded me of the time I got stung by a wasp and went into anaphylactic shock. These episodes also made me feel really sick to my stomach and caused a numb and tingly sensation in my head that started on the left side of my face near my cheeks and would travel up close to my temples. It was a feeling that I had never experienced before. I couldn't think straight, and I believe I came very close to passing out. The first time this happened to me I went straight to the emergency room because I thought for sure that I was having a stroke or something else was happening that could cause me to die.

They did a brain scan in the ER but couldn't find anything wrong. Although that was reassuring, I went home so confused about what was going on with my body. The episodes continued off and on for months and they wore me out. I was losing a lot of sleep and I had trouble functioning during the days that followed. I spent a lot of time and energy trying to figure out what was going on. I had allergy tests done because I thought maybe I was allergic to something that I was consuming or came in contact with. I even had extra tests done to see if I was sensitive to food dyes. Everything came back normal. I felt so confused. I asked my friends to pray for me and of course, I prayed and sought the Lord as well. I remember hearing Him telling me to get up and go for a walk. That was the last thing I wanted to do, but I found some relief in that. Healing doesn't always come as an instant change at a church revival. Sometimes God gives you one little step at a time to test your obedience. Maybe that's what He was doing with me when I listened and went for a walk.

As the years went on, the episodes became less frequent, but when they did happen, they were just as horrible as they were in the beginning. One of the scariest occurrences was about six years ago. My mother had recently had surgery on her brain to remove a tumor the size of a tennis ball. So, when these strange things started happening to my body again, I convinced myself that I had a tumor just like my mom. My state of panic led me to more hospital bills and time wasted and still no clear answers.

About a year had gone by since that episode and I almost forgot about this happening to me, but then it happened again. It was just before Christmas in 2017. On Christmas Eve, my head felt strange and then I suddenly felt a little light-headed. I got hot and sweaty, and my left arm started hurting. Then I made a huge mistake by googling my symptoms and I quickly convinced myself that I was having a heart attack or that there was a tumor in my brain (thinking of my mom again). From that point forward, for several months, I just wasn't doing well. My mind was overwhelmed with fear.

One night I woke up from a deep sleep and my entire body was shaking. My head felt strange (almost numb on one side) and fear consumed me. It was happening again, just like it used to! It took everything in me to not rush to the hospital again because it's a really scary thing to deal with in the middle of the night. My husband tried to help me calm down. He rubbed my back and told me that I was going to be okay. I pressed my nose against a bottle of massage oil that was meant to help relieve stress, and slowly and deeply inhaled the lavender scent as I tried my best to relax.

I began to speak II Timothy 1:7 over myself as I always would when I felt crippled by fear. This time, the words **"and a sound mind"** really stood out to me. For the first time, I understood I had not been living with a sound mind. A sound mind is full of peace, freedom, comfort, and joy! The opposite of a sound mind is anxiousness, fear, nervousness, sadness, and living in bondage. It was through seeing my favorite Bible verse in a new light that God revealed to me I had been having anxiety and panic attacks! I have no idea how all the doctors that I had seen over the years had completely missed that.

Are you living with a sound mind? If not, start speaking II Timothy 1:7 over your life. He has not given you a spirit of fear, but He has given you a sound mind!

If you're dealing with anxiety, I wish I could be there with you right now to give you a great, big hug. Anxiety is one of the loneliest roads I've ever had to walk. People look at you like you're a creature from another planet unless they've experienced anxiety for themselves. The way others responded to me when I tried to explain what I was going through, only made me feel more alone. But I promise you, you're not alone! That is exactly what Satan wants you to think. Don't be afraid to reach out to those around you to ask for help. Even if they don't understand, it helps to share your story because you give the enemy power by allowing anxiety to keep you isolated. You never know who else may be dealing with the same issues you are. Sharing your story with a trusted friend or family member may be the key to their freedom. If you can't bring yourself to talk to someone you know, then reach out to a professional. Just having someone listen to me without making me feel like I was crazy did so much for my mental health. If you do choose to reach out for professional help, be prayerful that the Lord will lead you to the right person to give you counsel. I always made sure to work with other Christians that have come highly recommended by those I trusted.

I know that sometimes the last thing you want to do is to drag yourself out of bed and face the world or even look at one more human being. But I'm telling you right now, **you will heal much quicker if you say enough is enough!** Even if you feel you just can't help it, the truth is that you can. Force yourself to get outside every single day, even if you call yourself an introvert (which by the way, is a title that you have given yourself and is not who the Lord says you are). Stop making excuses! I'm sorry if I sound harsh, but sometimes we need the real hard truth. Some fresh air and sunshine go a long way. If you're not in an area where the weather is nice, it can be helpful to just take a drive. Go window shopping or find something you enjoy to help take your mind off what is happening inside your mind. If all this just seems unbearable, I understand. I really do! If you have a friend who is willing to come visit you, try that for a start. ***Please though, don't isolate yourself from the rest of the world even though that's what your brain is telling you is best.***

Once I realized that my issues had a name, I went straight to Dr. Google (someday I'll learn my lesson) and started doing everything it suggested. Friend, Dr. Google doesn't have the answers for you. Sure, you might find some temporary relief, **but nothing compares to the total healing that can be found in Christ.** I tried so many things, mostly natural because I was afraid of the side effects of prescription medication. There were a couple of times I took prescription anxiety pills, but they just didn't work for me. One of them made me feel like a walking zombie. Yes, it took care of the anxiety, but I wasn't myself anymore. Each day was so foggy. I couldn't think straight, and I showed little to no emotion. It was like my mind was a blank screen. Another medication made me so sick that I got off it immediately. I figured anxiety was better than puking.

I took every good vitamin that I knew to take. Do you know that too much of a good thing can be bad for you? I took too many things on a daily basis. My body was all out of whack and some of it was my fault! I knew in my heart that there was an imbalance, so I prayed for God to give me wisdom and He pressed upon my heart to have my physician do complete blood work on me.

If you haven't had your blood drawn recently, I highly recommend getting it done. At my checkup I found out that I was extremely deficient in vitamin D and to my surprise, I learned that low vitamin D levels could contribute to anxiety. The day after I started taking a prescription-strength supplement, my heart stopped feeling like it was about to jump out of my chest and my resting heart rate went from the nineties to the sixties. I felt the most immediate relief that I've felt in years. Now don't take a high dose of vitamin D just because it worked for me because it could make things worse rather than better. Get the lab tests done to make sure you need it or else you could end up totally off balance like I was.

If you pray for God to give you wisdom, then don't miss your blessing by not being obedient in doing what He tells you to do. I would've never known that I had a vitamin deficiency if I hadn't heeded His advice. If you don't listen to Him, then that is probably the reason you are still living each day the same as the one before. We're meant to move forward and become all that Christ created us to be, not spend every day of our lives like a hamster running around on a wheel going nowhere. I fell into this trap when the Lord revealed to me I needed to stop taking medication for endometriosis, but I didn't listen.

For fifteen years I had been dealing with stage 3 endometriosis. As a teenager and in my early twenties, treatments for this horrible disease included several surgeries; two of which left me with scars that lined my lower stomach from one side to the other. I felt like a lab rat with all the different medications I tried to find some relief. I even had injections of one type of medication with irreversible side effects that lasted for months. I was so miserable! At just eighteen years old those shots put my body into a menopausal state. I felt like walking death but there was nothing I could do about it until it wore off about three months later.

Finally, the doctors put me on a medication that changed everything for me. For the first time since my diagnosis, I felt relief! Also, another plus for me (or so I thought) was that my periods were suppressed, so I didn't have to deal with that ever again.

In my mid-twenties I ended up needing surgery to have my gallbladder removed. Since I was already being cut open, I had my fertility specialist check everything out before they stitched my stomach back together. It was the best news I could've received! There was barely any endometriosis present, so that was more proof that my medication had been working. I continued the medication for several years, living a pain-free life.

I'll never forget the day that God told me to stop taking that medication. It was July 18, 2010. I attended a special conference at our church where Prophet Ed Traut was preaching. He called my husband and me out of the crowd and gave us an awesome word that I still stand on to this very day. Part of that prophecy was that I would write some books to help set people free. Sometimes when we are given a prophetic word, it's not meant for that very moment. It took me over eleven years to finally become a published author. I co-authored a children's book with my husband called, *Pushups and Crunches*. It's probably not a book that sets people free (although they will surely find joy in it), but it was a steppingstone that helped me realize I can accomplish whatever I put my mind to.

A prophetic word also usually takes work on your part. At the very least, you must guard your prophecy and keep it in mind as time goes on. I can't count how many times I revisit words that have been spoken over my life when I need direction from the Lord. Often when I do this, I find a missing piece to my life's puzzle. I couldn't make it fit at the time the word was delivered, but because many other pieces have since fallen into place, I can pick up that one piece that used to make no sense and see how it fits so perfectly now.

Prophet Traut also told me that God was going to use me and all the stuff that I've been through to make me a life source to the broken and the down and out. I would have techniques for bringing people out of abusive situations into a place of healing, fullness, wholeness, and wellness. He also said that God is using what the enemy thought he could destroy me with, to be a life source in my life. I know He is using this book to do just those things!

As the prophet finished speaking to us, he told me that as a sign that all of what he just said was true, when I got up from my seat, I would be healed. He said there was something in my stomach area that God has completely healed. I knew without a doubt that he was talking about the endometriosis.

I was extremely happy with the word that I received. I felt confirmation in my heart that the Lord had indeed healed me and that He wanted me to put all my trust in Him by getting off my medication. But guess what? I didn't want to stop taking it! Part of it was fear. Satan has a way of twisting things and making you question what you know the Lord said. He would whisper in my ear just as he did to Eve, "Are you sure God healed you?" With endometriosis, the only way to know for sure whether it's gone, is by having surgery. It is currently only visible to the human eye; there is no machine that can detect it. I would have to choose to believe that I was healed without being able to have any tests done to verify my healing. That felt like an ultimate test of my faith.

The other reason I didn't want to get off the medication was pure selfishness. Remember the part where I didn't have to deal with periods? I was enjoying my life without having to deal with that every month. But month after month, year after year, I kept hearing God's voice in my mind. "I have healed you. You need to stop taking that medication."

After EIGHT years, I decided to fully take that leap and trust God. Sadly, it wasn't just because I finally was obedient to Him. About five years ago, I had once again been dealing with anxiety and something inside of me just kept saying to go check my blood pressure. Aaron and I went to a local store where they had a blood pressure machine, and I was absolutely shocked to see the numbers 154/110! What on earth? My blood pressure had always been on the low side like my mom's. This is just another reminder to always listen to that voice in your mind that you know is God calling you to take action.

After researching to see if I needed to go to the hospital or not, I started wondering if it was possible that the medication I was taking for endometriosis could be the reason for the spike. Although it was highly unlikely, the mere chance of it being a possibility forced me to stop taking it.

I have to admit that I did struggle for several months just to get through my cycle. They were very heavy and painful. Some months I would doubt that I was really healed, but I kept declaring healing and standing on what I know He told me. I also asked for forgiveness for not being obedient from the moment that He told me to stop taking my medication. I couldn't help but wonder if I had listened sooner if things would've been easier for me. Although I had some tough months, everything continued to get easier and easier until eventually all the pain was gone, and my cycles were no longer heavy. Today I have zero issues, except for maybe craving too much chocolate!

I really wish I had listened to God all those years ago when He first healed me. There have been so many benefits that I never even considered. The biggest one is that I have been anxiety free for a few years now! Some of that was from my vitamin D prescription, but I believe that getting off my medication also helped. I have better skin and the spots on my face which were caused by my medication have slowly faded. I have more energy, my breasts stopped hurting (they had diagnosed me with fibrocystic breast disease), weight loss became easier, my headaches stopped, and my overall mood is so much better.

The craziest and most exciting change for me is that after about six months of being off the medication, I started noticing new hair growth all over my head. I've always had fine hair that fell out in clumps every time I would shower or blow dry it. After I had my babies, my hair fell out in patches and took forever to grow back. But since I stopped taking the medication, I am still finding new hair growth to this day. The proof is in the hair drying process which now takes me almost twice as long as it used to. I'm okay with that!

I encourage you to think back and ask the Lord if there's something He's told you to do that you've not yet done. It could be anything big or small. Sometimes you can't move forward toward the big things in life because you haven't done the small things He's told you to do. As I reflect on my days of living with anxiety, it's as if I was walking around just existing, nothing more. Anxiety keeps you in your own personal jail cell where you can't see beyond the walls that confine you. There's a whole new world full of freedom and adventure, but you must find a way to tear down those prison bars.

REFLECT

Could disobedience be the reason you are still bound by the chains of anxiety? Is there something in your life that you know the Lord has told you to do, but you just haven't done it yet? If we're honest with ourselves, there's usually *something* that we've missed along the way. Maybe you were supposed to finish getting your degree, move away (or move back home), start a business, or write a book. Or maybe it's something that He's told you to stop doing, like smoking or quitting some other bad habit. Has He told you to cut off toxic relationships, stop gossiping, or stop watching shows that don't glorify Him?

There are so many things that it could be. If something doesn't come to you immediately, take some time to pause and ask the Holy Spirit for help. Ask God to remind you of anything in your life that could keep you from moving forward. Ask Him if there's any area of your life where you have been disobedient to Him. If the answer is yes, then He has handed you the key to your freedom, and that key is to repent and to decide right now that you will walk forward in obedience to Him from this point forward.

One thing I've struggled with lately is completing this book. Day after day I can feel the Lord pressing me to work on it, but I've made excuse after excuse. God has been faithful to keep me going though. Recently, an old friend shared with me that she gave her life to Christ and that I'm the one who planted the seed a couple of years ago. I asked her if she could remember anything that really stuck with her, and she said it was when I shared my story about being freed from fear. That conversation with her was enough to make me sit at the computer again to work on this book. If one discussion could lead a friend to Christ, then I can only imagine what this book can do. I know it's an assignment from the Lord and I pray it blesses your life tremendously. I also trust that the mission He's given you will spill over as a great resource into others' lives. Keep pressing forward and one day you will see the fruit of your labor and obedience. Feel free to log below anything that the Holy Spirit brings to your mind that may be keeping you from moving forward.

My Reflections

CHAPTER FIVE

THE ROOT OF ALL FEARS

One day God gave me another revelation that really helped me with anxiety and fear. He showed me that the root of every single fear in my life was the fear of dying.

My eyes had suddenly been opened to see that I had many fears rooted in the fear of death. These fears literally kept me from leaving my house. I would fear exposing my kids to germs and diseases that could ultimately kill them, and that was long before coronavirus existed. I also stayed home because I feared being involved in an act of terrorism. All over the world, I would hear about another school shooting, shootings in malls and movie theaters, people being hit by cars in crowds by a crazy terrorist, and large cities being bombed during special events.

The more I prayed about these things, the more I could see that it is not God's will for His people to crouch back and stay hidden from the world. God spoke to my heart and said that it didn't matter if I stayed home where I felt safe or if I went out into the world daily. My steps are ordered by Him and that is something I cannot change. Psalm 37:23 says, "The steps of a good man are ordered by the LORD, and He delights in his way."

One day the Lord told me I could be sitting at home minding my own business and a plane could crash above me and kill me on the spot. Or someone can break into our home and take my life. You would think that this would increase anxiety, but it truly gave me a strong sense of peace; A peace knowing that I can relax. God is in complete control, not only of my life, but yours too! Morris West put it best when he said, *"If you spend your whole life inside waiting for the storms, you'll never enjoy the sunshine."* How much truth is in that?

God wants to bless you beyond what your mind can even imagine. II Corinthians 9:8 (NIV) says, "And God is able to bless you abundantly, so that in all things at all times, having all that you need, you will abound in every good work." Did you catch that word, *abundantly*? Although it is His desire to abundantly bless us, we'll miss out on so much if we allow fear to lead our decisions. I cannot imagine how much more adventurous my life would have been if I weren't afraid of dying. Even though I spent over forty years of my life missing out on God's best plans for me, I praise Him for giving me a word that would change the course of the rest of my life.

I can't remember exactly what I was worrying about, but I remember clearly when I heard a gentle whisper from the Lord.

He said that He already knows when and how I will take my last breath. That is not for me to know, but I can't spend the rest of my life worrying about it.

I have always believed that God knows every detail of our lives, including our exact time of death, but hearing Him speak about it directly to my heart brought new comfort to my soul and I finally stopped worrying about dying. It really changes things when you hear it from the Lord Himself instead of from another human being.

Luke 12:25 (NIV) says, "Who of you by worrying can add a single hour to your life?" The Passion Translation says it like this, "Does worry add anything to your life? Can it add one more year or even one day? (v26) So if worrying adds nothing, but actually subtracts from your life, why would you worry about God's care of you?"

Worrying doesn't change what God has already determined for your life! It only causes your life to be more miserable.

One of my biggest triggers for fear and anxiety used to be storms. Unless this has been a troublesome area for you, you would probably think that I was completely nuts because of the way storms had me in such bondage. Now that I am free from fear, I am blown away at how I behaved!

If the news showed the slightest risk for severe weather in the forecast or even just a marginal risk, I would completely shut down. Even if bad weather was projected for three days away, my mind would immediately go into a fog, and I could no longer function like normal. I couldn't eat or sleep and it was like my brain would just stop working. I was terrified of being alone in storms too. If I knew my husband wouldn't be home when the storms were predicted, I went into panic mode. I was also much more afraid when I lived in homes that didn't have a basement. I was absolutely terrified that a tornado was going to come and kill me and our children. See, there's that main root of all my fears again.

Many of my friends were well accustomed to my irrational behavior during storms. Days before the bad weather was approaching, I would text certain friends (the ones with the basements) to ask if I could come stay with them until the storms passed. When no one messaged me back (because they were probably thinking I was insane), I put out a plea on Facebook. I'm just trying to paint a picture for you of just how serious this was for me. It was absolutely life-altering.

I realize that not everyone will have the same root of fear as I had. What is it for you? Is it fear of failure, rejection, fear of making a mistake, or a fear of living in poverty? Is it fear of becoming who you used to be? Are you worried about what others think of you and allow their opinions to rule your life? Or is it something else?

It's likely that once you discover the deepest-rooted seed of fear, it will help you better understand why you think and behave the way you do.

What do you do when you finally discover what the main root of all your fears is? The first thing to do is repent. Ask the Lord for forgiveness for all the times that you allowed fear to rule in your life. Second, command the most deeply rooted fear and everything attached to it to be broken off your life. God has given you authority through Jesus Christ to use your mouth to destroy the enemy's power that has been at work. While we're on the subject of using your mouth, you must watch what you are speaking if you truly want to be set free from bondage. The Bible says in Proverbs 18:21, "Death and life are in the power of the tongue, and those who love it will eat its fruit." Essentially what you are speaking over your life is the harvest that you are going to get. If you are dealing with an illness, instead of saying, "I keep feeling worse every day," or "My back is killing me," start prophesying over your body and say things like, "By His stripes, I am healed," or "I can do all things through Christ who strengthens me."

Now that I know that my deepest root of fear is the fear of dying, I can start speaking against that. I can say out loud that I am not afraid to die. Declare it! Say, "I renounce the fear of _____ in the name of Jesus." Start paying more attention to the words that come out of your mouth. Are you speaking blessing or cursing over your life?

Just like you can't plant apple seeds and expect to grow a peach tree, you can't keep planting negative words against your life and expect healing, restoration, prosperity, or peace.

When you plant good seeds, you reap the fruit of the Spirit which is love, joy, peace, long-suffering, kindness, goodness, faithfulness, gentleness, and self-control.

If you are cursing your own life with your words, can you imagine what others might be doing on your behalf? Most of them don't even intend to harm you, but it could be happening daily, and you don't even realize it. You better be very careful whom you share your situation with. When you call up your brother or sister in Christ or that family member and ask them to pray for you, they might pray for you, but they also might be planting negative seeds on your behalf. Once the phone call is over, they may get into a conversation with others and say things like, "Did you hear about sister Robin? She's really sick." Even though they prayed for you, they go on to speak sickness over your life.

Be prayerful about whom you share your circumstances with, but as an extra layer of protection, you may want to try something that I often practice. All spoken words are seeds that have been planted. So at least on a weekly basis, I pray for God to destroy every negative seed that has been planted on my behalf, whether by myself or others, and I ask Him to only allow the good seeds to be nourished and to turn into a harvest.

Another way to combat your deepest fears is to meditate on relevant scriptures. The Bible is full of God's promises to us. I guarantee that no matter what you are dealing with, there is a helpful scripture to help bring peace to your soul.

- If you are afraid of becoming poor or experiencing financial trouble, speak out Psalm 34:10, "...those who seek the LORD shall not lack any good thing."
- If it's a fear of failure, speak out Philippians 4:13, "I can do all things through Christ who strengthens me."
- If your deepest root is the fear of dying, speak out I John 4:18 (MSG), "There is no room in love for fear.

Well-formed love banishes fear. Since fear is crippling, a fearful life - fear of death, fear of judgment - is one not yet fully formed in love."

If you are unsure of what Bible verse to use, a simple search on the internet can help you. Just type in "Bible verse that combats the fear of _____." Continually speak the verse or verses out loud; not just until you have it memorized, but until you begin to fully believe what the Bible says about your fears and until you have gained the peace that surpasses all understanding.

Another thing that really helped me is something I read or heard somewhere, and it stuck with me. It was the saying, ***"Don't be so afraid of dying that you become afraid to live."*** We only have one shot at this life. Don't waste it! Whatever that deeply rooted fear is, you need to decide today that you will no longer allow it to keep you from living life to the fullest.

REFLECT

Think about your biggest fears. *Is it possible that the fear of death is also the root of all your other fears?* If not, then what is it? If you're unsure, then take some time to get quiet with the Holy Spirit and ask Him to show you what that root is.

What happens when you pull a tree up by the roots? It dies! When you can see clearly what the largest root of fear is in your life, then you will know exactly what you need to start pulling and tugging on until it has been completely removed from your life. Once you pull out that main root, all the other branches will die.

Use the cover of this book for inspiration and picture your own "tree of fear". Imagine the main large root buried deep beneath the surface. Then see all the different branches attached to that giant tree. For me, the fear of dying would be the largest root. It was always there, but I just couldn't see it because it was buried underneath all the other more obvious fears. Those are my branches; fear of going out in public, fear of storms, fear of getting stung by a bee, fear of being misunderstood or unwanted, fear of failure and so on. If you're artistic, maybe a great exercise for you would be to draw or paint your tree, labeling the roots and each branch.

As you bring this image to life in your mind or on canvas, things will begin to change because you now clearly understand what really needs to be destroyed. Once that main root is gone, all remaining fears will have lost their life source.

My Reflections

CHAPTER SIX

A LIFE RUINED WITH REGRET

Right before I finally broke completely free of fear, I had an opportunity of a lifetime, yet I allowed fear to take over all my thoughts. My husband earned a completely free trip to Playa Del Carmen, Mexico for the two of us. When he first told me about the trip, he didn't get the reaction he was expecting. Instead of being overwhelmed with joy, I was completely overtaken with fear and anxiety. What was supposed to be a romantic moment with a spectacular surprise, turned into me almost having a panic attack right there in our hot tub.

The what ifs immediately started playing over and over in my mind. Day and night my own thoughts tormented me. What if the plane crashed and our children were left without parents? Who would take care of them if we died? Our youngest was about three years old at the time. I wondered if he would even remember me. What if our kids got sick or hurt while we were gone, or their caregiver got in an accident with them? What if the roads were bad on the way to the airport? On and on and on my mind would race, until one night I broke down and told Aaron that I just couldn't go because every time I thought about it, panic set in and I felt like I was being suffocated.

I have a wonderful husband who tried his best to understand what I was going through, but frustration almost got the best of him, and he came very close to not going on his well-deserved trip. Eventually, and reluctantly on his part, we came to an agreement that he would go, and I would stay home with the boys. I really thought that I was happy with my choice because I instantly felt such relief. It felt like the anxiety was flushed down the drain and a heavy weight was lifted with my decision to stay home.

I had such peace leading up to the trip, but when the day came for Aaron to leave, I immediately regretted my decision. It seemed like the very moment he left, I became emotionally unstable, and my thoughts turned to resentment and anger. Have you ever wallowed in pity because of a decision that you made? That's where I was. It's bad enough when you don't have a choice, but when you realize you made the wrong decision, the guilt piles up on top of all the other emotions that you feel. That week seemed like one of the worst weeks of my life. I came down with a cold, couldn't sleep, chipped a tooth, and our children behaved exceptionally badly. Sickness amplified all the negative emotions I was dealing with, but somehow, I was able to push through all the chaos. I cried and prayed for God to forgive me and help me. I begged Him to give me another chance.

As I sat in church that Sunday, I felt like our pastor was preaching directly to me when he said,

"If you live in the what-ifs, you'll live a life that is ruined with regret."

My husband was on the trip of a lifetime, and I was miserable because I had allowed all the what-ifs to have control over my decisions. Tears streamed down my face as I vowed to the Lord that I was done living a life full of regret. Again, I asked Him to give me another chance. I was ready to face my fears as I realized fears come and go but regret will last forever.

Our pastor also said something that I believe caused a shift in my life, but it only shifted because I was obedient to the revelation. He said, ***"When God reveals something to you that requires an action, you must act quickly because if you don't, that's disobedience!"*** Pastor Brent Ireland also said that generosity starts at 11% and generosity will never let you stay where you are. Aaron and I have always been faithful tithers, but I knew I needed to begin tithing at least 11% from that day forward, so that's exactly what I did. I didn't want to stay stuck in the life that I had been living, bound by fear and anxiety, and missing out on God's amazing plans for my future. I stood on the words that our pastor had spoken, AND THE VERY NEXT DAY GOD PROVIDED ME WITH THAT SECOND CHANCE THAT I ASKED HIM FOR!

The day after church, Aaron called me from Mexico. He sounded nervous as he told me about an opportunity that had come up. The owner of his company asked him if he and I would be interested in taking a trip to New Orleans the following month. Aaron had no idea what had happened at church the day before, so he really didn't think I would want to go because we would have to fly to get there. He told me how amazing the trip would be and then he said to think about it and let him know my decision soon. Well, as soon as we hung up the phone, I sent him a text that said, "I'll go." I imagine he had to rub his eyes a few times and make sure he was seeing things clearly since he was unaware of the work that the Lord had just done in my life.

Fast forward to just one month later and there we were in New Orleans. We ate dinner at a Brazilian steakhouse and then we got to see my husband's favorite band, NEEDTOBREATHE. After the concert we got to go backstage for a meet and greet. The favor and blessings from God that night were just so overwhelming. And talk about facing my fears! I had to get on four flights in a twenty-four-hour period; one of which took off during a storm.

Once I realized God had given me another chance, it was literally like a veil had been torn from my eyes. I got mad at the devil! I finally saw that I really made the wrong choice by not going to Mexico with Aaron. My priorities were all out of whack. It's not supposed to be kids first, everyone else second, and me dead last! I failed to put the Lord first and my husband second, while taking care of myself. I'm imagining so many people reading this right now who can also admit that their priorities are out of order because this is such an issue in our world. When is the last time in your life that you truly put God first? Honestly, He doesn't just want first place, He wants to be your everything. Oswald Chambers put it perfectly when he said, "Your priorities must be God first, God second, and God third, until your life is continually face to face with God."

Something else happened in my life around this time that shifted me away from a lifetime of regret. I turned forty years old, and I realized I had lived the first twenty years of my life trying to please my dad. He always compared me to my older brothers and if they failed in any area, he told me I would do the same as they did. I wasn't even allowed to mention graduating high school since my brothers always said they were going to graduate but they didn't. My brothers had a much tougher life than I did during high school, so it is understandable why they didn't get their diplomas.

Instead of just giving up on everything, I took an "I'll show him" attitude toward my dad. Although that pushed me to finish high school, land a great job, and begin my journey in college, it was all done as an effort to prove myself to my dad. Finishing high school was something I always knew that I would do, but I had planned to become a teacher. Although I'm grateful for my dad helping me to get on at the company he worked for, it changed the entire course of my future. The company paid my way through school as long as it was work-related. I just couldn't pass up on that deal, so I changed my major from teaching to business with a focus on management.

I wanted to sing. I wanted to teach. And I wanted to be a mom. Those were my ultimate goals in life. But I allowed other people and circumstances to get me off track. Thank God for His mercy and His plans because I ended up dropping out of college my senior year (I have no regrets by the way), marrying the man of my dreams, having children, and staying home to teach them. God allowed me to teach without having a degree! I never dreamed that it would be my own children that I would be teaching, but I'm so blessed that He chose them to be my students.

Trying to please my dad turned into bigger issues because without even realizing it, I became the ultimate people pleaser. I said yes to every demand because I was too worried about hurting someone's feelings or fearing that they wouldn't like me. I don't know how many times I ended up feeling angry and frustrated after going out of my way to please someone whom I didn't even really care for, all because I had guilted myself into it. I never wanted to let *anyone* down. I also worried that they would think less of me if I told them no.

While I spent the first twenty years of my life trying to please my dad and everyone else, the next twenty years were centered on my children. We were years into our marriage before Aaron and I spent more than a night away from our first son; and even that one-night trip only happened a time or two. I quit my job to homeschool and that was okay because it made me happy, but I also stopped doing things for myself, and somewhere along the way I stopped singing. Isn't it crazy how easily mothers bury their own dreams to take care of their children? It's not something that usually happens overnight, but little by little, they fade away until you don't even remember what it was like to dream your own dreams.

I looked in the mirror and realized that I had spent the last FORTY YEARS living life for other people! Yes, we are supposed to be God's servants, but He doesn't intend for us to NEVER put ourselves first!

Are you a people pleaser? Do you realize that the root of being a people pleaser is fear? It's time to rise up and tune your ears to what God almighty has told you to do with your life and stop worrying about what everyone else thinks or what everyone else is expecting you to do. Your assignment from the Lord comes with an expiration date! You won't be on this planet forever. If you waste your time trying to make everyone else happy, you could end up missing the fullness of life that Jesus died to give you. Look at King Saul. In I Samuel, chapter fifteen, the Lord had commanded Saul to destroy all the Amalekites and their belongings, but he was disobedient to God because he feared the people more than he trusted in God's plans. This ended up costing him the throne!

What have you lost by living your life to please others? Whatever it may be, God is a redeemer and if you focus more on the calling He has placed on your life and less on what others *think* you should do, I believe you will start enjoying life more. This doesn't mean that we turn into selfish people. It's more likely that as we do the work that God has placed in our hearts, we will be serving and loving others in the process.

The Sunday after our trip to New Orleans, I went to church and everything that I had been experiencing came together for me. There was no preaching whatsoever because once the worship had ended my pastor felt led by the Holy Spirit to pray over each person there. He was praying for a release, and that is exactly what I got! I went in with a band-aid of fear just dangling from my eyebrow. As he prayed over me, that final piece was ripped away from my life forever.

Now I feel amazing, light, and carefree! I feel a peace that makes no sense in the natural. It's the kind of peace that I've always read about in Philippians 4:7, "And the peace of God, which surpasses all understanding, will guard your hearts and minds through Christ Jesus."

The Lord has also helped me to use the word "no" more often. Just because you are a Christian doesn't mean that you have to say yes to everything that is asked of you. In fact, the more I say no to other people's demands, the more clearly I see the Lord and *His* plans for my life. It's like God has extremely narrowed my focus and that lens is directed straight toward Him. When you spend more time in God's Word, you get to know Him better. As your relationship with Him gets stronger, so does your discernment, and that is how you know which things you should say yes to and which ones you shouldn't.

I know that all the blessings I've experienced are nothing but God's goodness toward me. I cried out to Him, and He heard me! *How my heart is saddened by all the opportunities I've missed, but greater is the joy that I'm experiencing as I move forward with my arms open and ready to receive all that He has for me!*

Fear ran so much deeper than I can explain. I was in serious bondage, but God made a way for me. I want you to know that because He did it for me, that just means that He can do it for you too! Romans 2:11 says, "For there is no partiality with God." Stand strong on His promises. Keep confessing His Word over your life. Praise Him even when you feel you have no reason to praise Him. If you can get to that point, I promise you that there will be a breakthrough for you. I don't know how long it will take; I only know that it is possible! In Matthew 19:26 Jesus says, "With men this is impossible, but with God all things are possible."

REFLECT

What opportunities have you missed out on because of fear? What are some of the what-ifs that play over and over in your mind? Ask the Lord to take away all the bad scenarios that play out in your mind and to replace them with His thoughts; thoughts that are true, noble, just, pure, lovely, of good report, virtuous and praiseworthy.

> *Finally, brethren, whatever things are true, whatever things are noble, whatever things are just, whatever things are pure, whatever things are lovely, whatever things are of good report, if there is any virtue and if there is anything praiseworthy—meditate on these things. Philippians 4:8*

My Reflections

CHAPTER SEVEN

WISDOM OR FEAR?

I wrote most of the previous chapters a few years ago because the Lord had me pause my writing to focus on other things. During that time, I experienced some of the most amazing moments of my life so far. Aaron and I wrote a children's book, I took a trip to Florida with my aunt and my boys to visit my parents, and Aaron earned another all-inclusive trip. This time it was to Jamaica!

I faced all the what-ifs that I was too afraid to face when he had earned his trip to Mexico. I'm so grateful to God that I overcame the fears that had loomed in my mind for over forty years because Jamaica was an incredible place! Because I pushed through the fears, I got to see the most beautiful ocean, I made some great friends, and I got to hike up a breathtaking waterfall. To get to the waterfall, I had to face the fear of allowing someone else to drive. We rode in a bus for over an hour from our hotel to get there. It was strange to me too, since the driver is on the opposite side than what I am used to. Although I was a little nervous, I knew I was in God's hands and that He was so happy to show off other parts of His creation that I would have never seen if I had chosen to remain bound by fear.

Guess what else happened over the last few years? The entire world experienced a pandemic. Prior to the pandemic, I thought I had been walking in freedom, but the truth became obvious during the winter months. I had made progress in so many ways, but I missed a ton of church because I was still worried about my children getting the flu. I always stayed home during cold and flu season just to be safe. I thought I was using wisdom.

But in February 2020, the Lord revealed to me I was once again living in fear and then He reminded me that there is nothing I can do by my own strength to keep my family from getting sick. Again, He said to me, "Amanda, your last earthly day has already been determined. Don't question it and don't waste any more time worrying about it." My heart was immediately convicted, and I knew what I had to do.

As that last bit of film was finally removed from my spiritual eyes, I became determined that I wouldn't miss another day of church unless one of us was sick, and even then, I may have to take the sick one to the church for prayer. Isn't the church supposed to be a place for the sick? I'll never forget the look of complete surprise on Pastor Brent's face when I showed up one Sunday after a worldwide pandemic had been declared, but I hadn't been showing up because of the flu! My new life felt kind of surreal. People knew it was really me because my body looked the same, but my countenance changed. I no longer just showed up for church, I came wearing a garment of praise.

As I stepped into my brand-new life, I noticed so many people around me entering the life that I had just come from. How ironic! My heart cried out to everyone who was going in the opposite direction, "No, don't go that way! It's a trap. I've been there for over forty years, and it only leads to captivity. Turn around! Please!" Oh, how my heart aches for everyone who is still bound by the chains brought on by the pandemic. It's as if they don't even realize that they are being weighed down and held back from a beautiful, free life!

A couple of months after the pandemic began, I was preparing to give my testimony at church about how God freed me from fear. The night before I was to speak, the Lord woke me up out of my sleep and told me to tell the people to **stop confusing wisdom with fear.** Just as I had once thought that I was being wise by keeping my family home during flu season, now people all over the globe mistakenly believed that they were being wise by avoiding other people, and even worse, avoiding church.

Friend, it is Satan's plan to get you isolated. He has used the pandemic just like he has used anxiety and depression to separate you from the people that God intended to be in your life. Many people became too comfortable staying home, and they still have no desire to get back to church. That was the enemy's plan all along! He also used that season to bring offense to the hearts of God's people. Perhaps you are one who felt hurt when no one seemed to notice when you stopped showing up. If you're still not back in church, you have made the devil proud.

Satan also used the pandemic to bring disunity. It saddens me how easily we all fell for it, hating our brothers and sisters over their opinions on masks and vaccines. I'm not going to lie; I've been judgmental too. It's been difficult for me to feel such freedom and not allow it to turn into pride. I've had to remind myself of where I was not too long ago. I praise God for rescuing me because I cannot imagine what the last few years would've been like if He hadn't completely freed me from fear and anxiety. My heart breaks for those of you who had to go through it completely alone and fearful. Know that I have prayed for you, and I want you to experience the freedom and joy I have found.

Wisdom doesn't always make sense in the natural. Proverbs 12:15 says, "The way of a fool is right in his own eyes, but he who heeds counsel is wise." I'm not accusing you of being a fool, it's just that sometimes we think we have it all figured out when really, we don't even have a clue. Do you ever look back on your life and laugh at the plans you once had? I thought I would find the love of my life, get married, have four babies (two boys and two girls, maybe even a set of twins), and live happily ever after. Ha! The Lord blessed me with four babies, but it wasn't in my ideal way or the timing that I would've chosen to bring them into this world. I also planned to have all-natural births. I even believed for supernatural, pain-free childbirths. That sure didn't go as I planned! Three of the four births were emergency cesareans. One thing is for sure though, since I have experienced raising four boys, I'm glad he didn't give me the twins I was hoping for! Whew! Parents of multiples, you are truly amazing people. I'm sure your children are complete blessings, but I feel exhausted just imagining taking care of more than one baby at a time. Two in diapers at the same time was enough for me.

God knows what He's doing. No matter how much I tried and prayed for a girl, He created me to be a boy mom. We try to figure everything out, but it's His plans for our lives that will prevail. Why do we waste so much time worrying about how things will turn out? The only thing that truly matters at the end of the day is where we and our loved ones will spend eternity after we take our last breath. Even when you turn your plans over to the Lord, there will always be new decisions in life that will require action from you. Let's say you are offered a new job or you're not sure if you should move. How do you base your decision on wisdom and not be driven by fear? If you allow fear to drive your decisions, you will be headed straight for disaster. The second part of Proverbs 12:15 says that the wise heed counsel. Have you taken your plans to a trusted friend or leader in your church? A couple of years ago Aaron and I thought about moving to Florida. Before that it was Georgia. Both times, our pastor's wife told us she just didn't think it was the right time. Turns out that she was right. It's always a good idea to share your plans with people whom you know you can trust; people who won't just tell you what you want to hear. It's even better if whomever you go to has the gift of discernment.

How else can you be sure that you are walking in wisdom and not in the flesh? What I'm going to tell you seems so obvious, but so many people just don't do it. You need to test the scriptures. Are you living your life according to the Word? There is a Bible verse for almost every imaginable situation that you will face.

I reflect on when I thought I was being wise by keeping my kids home during cold and flu season. I wonder how I ever thought for a moment that the Lord would prefer that I keep my perfectly healthy children home in an effort to protect them, instead of taking them to church? Do you realize how ridiculous that really is? I know I'm going to ruffle some feathers, but the Lord never told healthy people to stay home. Where in the Bible does it say, "Stay home ye healthy people for there you are safe from sickness and disease?" That is nowhere to be found! But you know what you will find?

Is anyone among you sick? Let him call for the elders of the church, and let them pray over him, anointing him with oil in the name of the Lord. James 5:14

This is not the time to pull away and neglect meeting together, as some have formed the habit of doing. In fact, we should come together even more frequently, eager to encourage and urge each other onward as we anticipate that day dawning. Hebrews 10:25 (TPT)

But seek first the kingdom of God and His righteousness, and all these things shall be added to you. Therefore do not worry about tomorrow, for tomorrow will worry about its own things. Sufficient for the day is its own trouble. Matthew 6:33-34

Therefore take heed to yourselves and to all the flock, among which the Holy Spirit has made you overseers, to shepherd the church of God which He purchased with His own blood. Acts 20:28

And do not be conformed to this world, but be transformed by the renewing of your mind, that you may prove what is that good and acceptable and perfect will of God. Romans 12:2

For where two or three are gathered together in My name, I am there in the midst of them. Matthew 18:20

God created us for community! Keep seeking Him above all else and continue gathering with your brothers and sisters in Christ. Don't become so comfortable missing church that it becomes hard to find your way back. If you've already found yourself in this position, I challenge you to just go back for one day. I have a feeling that it will leave you longing for more!

Back when I was bound by fear, I was reading my Bible often, I prayed a lot, and I attended church almost every Sunday, but I still stayed home during the winters because I was scared. If you feel you are doing all the right things spiritually yet you're still living a life bound by fear, anxiety, or depression, I just want to tell you to not give up. True freedom is possible, and I am living proof!

If you are a Christian, you shouldn't be questioning whether you are walking in wisdom because you know in your spirit if you are free or bound. The Lord will convict you if you are open to hear His voice. **The real question is, do you have the courage to make a change?** I honestly knew that I was making decisions based on fear, but I used wisdom as a coverup and an excuse. How naïve I was to think for one second I could protect my children better than God could!

What would your life look like if fear wasn't a factor? I once asked myself this same question back when I was bound by fear.

Here's what I wrote in my journal in 2014:
How would a fear-free life differ from the life I have today?

- *I would take my kids out in public more often, put the baby in the nursery at church, be more committed to homeschool groups, and invite more people into our home.*
- *I would not be afraid of us getting sick.*
- *I would be able to enjoy the summer, not worrying about getting stung.*
- *I would never get sick because of the weather forecasts.*
- *I would travel more and even take trips on airplanes. I would get to see more of God's beautiful creation.*
- *I would sleep better at night, not worrying about my children.*
- *I would allow our oldest son to babysit the other boys so I could enjoy more freedom.*
- *I wouldn't be fearful when I'm driving, which would allow me to relax and enjoy the drive.*
- *I wouldn't be afraid of something happening to Aaron or the boys.*

After I wrote all these possibilities, I questioned whether fear was causing me to live a safe, but boring life. Doesn't it seem like life would be so much more exciting if we could conquer the things that make us fearful instead of constantly trying to hide from them?

Special prayer for anyone feeling confused regarding wisdom and fear:

Father God, I pray for the person reading this right now. Break off every lie that the enemy has spoken over them. Reveal it and break it in the name of Jesus! I pray that Your truth will be poured into the crevices of their spirit that once harbored the lies of Satan. Show them any area of their life where they may be using wisdom as a cover-up for fear. Expose EVERY AREA of fear in their life that the enemy has twisted in their minds, causing them to believe that those fears are actually good things. I pray You increase their discernment so they will always know Your truth from lies. Bless them with real wisdom and revelation in the areas where they need it the most. Help them God to stop living a safe but boring life. Reveal to them the beauty and adventure that awaits them if they would just put their full trust in You. Help them to truly rest, knowing that You are in total control of their life and that You love them with a love that can't be experienced with any human being on earth. I pray that if they have experienced hurt by their earthly parents, You will show them You are a Father that will never leave them nor forsake them and that Your plans for them are great! Show them You are for them, not against them. Help them draw closer to You day by day. Show them they are more than a conqueror and there is no fear too big for You to destroy. Give them the clarity and courage that they need to make the necessary changes to move forward in life instead of forever being held back by the chains of fear and anxiety. I ask You to do these things quickly and completely so that they can taste the freedom that You've blessed me with and so that their life will be a living testimony to those who know them. In Jesus's name I pray, Amen.

REFLECT

Is it possible that you have mistaken fear for wisdom? Have you bought into the lie that it's safer to remain at home? While you are snuggled up in your cocoon, someone else is out there living an adventurous life. What do you have to gain by staying isolated? Do you believe God is always with you? If so, what is it that's holding you back from living a life full of purpose?

Take a few moments and get honest with yourself. Ask yourself how your life would be different if fear wasn't a factor. Write out your list and pray over it. Ask God to help you face those fears so you can live your best life.

My Reflections

CHAPTER EIGHT

DEPRESSION

I want to touch on depression a little because it goes hand in hand with fear and anxiety. If you are depressed, it can lead to anxiety and fear, and if you're dealing with anxiety and fear, it can lead to depression. It's like a vicious cycle that's hard to escape. Proverbs 12:25 (TPT) says, "Anxious fear brings depression, but a life-giving word of encouragement can do wonders to restore joy to the heart." So according to the Bible, anxiety and fear bring depression, but I hope this book is a life-giving word of encouragement to you that will help bring restoration.

My first hard battle with depression came when I was only sixteen years old. This is the absolute hardest part of this book for me to write because it is my biggest kept secret. I've been holding this in for over twenty-seven years. I don't want to write it. I don't want my family to know about it. But I know that there is someone out there who needs to know; someone who can relate and understand that they are not alone.

My life as a teenager was okay. High school was rough, but I tried my best to stay true to myself and not allow anyone else to change me, even though I was the constant target of bullying just because kids were mean, and they needed someone to pick on. I handled the bullying as well as I could, but then something happened that just broke me. I was dating someone who I thought was so cool because he was a little older than me. In the beginning, he treated me very well. I also developed a good relationship with his sisters, and I would fantasize about being a part of their family one day. I thought he was something else because he was the first guy whom I rode in a car with. I can't remember if my parents allowed that or if I snuck and met him places and then got in the car with him. I had my license too because I remember driving myself to work where he and I worked together.

All the warm and fuzzy thoughts that I had about this boy suddenly came to a halt one day when we found ourselves alone at his house and he forced me to have sex with him. That was just the beginning of many forced moments I can't bear to talk about, yet there I was, afraid to leave him. I felt like it didn't matter if I stayed with him or not because the damage was already done, and I really didn't know how to leave him without someone discovering what had happened. Somehow, I felt like I deserved it for allowing myself to be alone with him in the first place. I blamed myself for so many years.

My innocence had been stolen. I had planned to save myself for marriage, but from the first time that he raped me, I instantly felt dirty and developed a low sense of self-worth. I was afraid to tell anyone. My initial thoughts were that I would be in so much trouble, but more than that, I felt like my parents would look at me differently; the way I had started seeing myself. I felt like I had let everyone down in the biggest possible way. The worst is how I thought God probably felt about me. My biggest reason for wanting to save myself for marriage was because I wanted to please God and now I felt like even the Lord Himself must be so disappointed in me. There was something else that happened that made me want to stay silent. Without going into details, something happened to one of my brothers when I was younger, by a man whom my family trusted. I saw the torment that came from that situation, and I didn't want to cause any more heartache for my family.

That was the beginning of depression for me; the beginning of feeling hopeless and feeling like my life didn't matter anymore. Since I had experienced an alcoholic dad, the situation with my brother, and then having my innocence stolen at such a young age, I started believing that all men were evil. Trust has been the hardest thing for men to earn in my life because of the brokenness I have experienced in the past.

It took me growing up and realizing that telling that boy no on every occasion is what made it **not** my fault. Even though I had come to grips with what had happened, it left a scar on my heart. No, it left an open wound that only God could repair and writing about it now feels like the last step to true healing, a final act of letting go.

Fast forward to just four years later when I was twenty years old. My son was just one year old, and I was struggling to understand why God would bless me with a child, only for his father to take the easy way out and leave us to figure out life on our own. Looking back though, I can see that my sin was a big factor in all of that. I was so focused on wanting to have a baby that I didn't really care who it was with, nor did I care I wasn't married. This all stems from the pains of my past and being told that I may never be able to have children. Thank God for His mercy, forgiveness, and grace. I can see now that He protected me and blessed me through the struggles that I faced as a single mom.

The Lord is a redeemer full of grace and mercy, but when you strive so hard to get your own way, ignoring the Biblical instructions for life, you're setting yourself up for disaster. Year after year I dated all the wrong men. It seemed like they only wanted one thing and most of them left me soon after they got what they wanted. Again, I honestly believed that all men were just pigs, and no one would ever truly care for me the way I hoped. So many nights I would throw myself on my bed and cry my eyes out. I blamed God for not sending me a good father for my son. There was a time when

I screamed out loud, "I hate You God!" I'll never forget the way I felt in that moment: empty, broken, used, unwanted, unloved.

I turned to alcohol to numb the emotional pain. I would leave my son with my parents so I could go out partying. I just wanted to feel something good. Alcohol didn't make me feel good though. In fact, it made me feel worse. I never named it back then, but I was depressed. Depression led me to alcohol and alcohol led me to a whole other prison. There was more shame, more guilt, and more thoughts of failure.

Just like that, I had become an alcoholic. I don't know if my family knows this about me, so it's yet another part of my life that is extremely difficult to write. It hurts to think that I fell into the same category as so many others in my family. How did I let that happen, knowing what alcohol did to my dad and my brothers? I'm even guilty of drinking and driving. I'm just blessed that I never got caught and nothing terrible happened because of my ignorance. I question how I got there too, knowing what happened to my mother. Several years ago, she could've easily been killed by a drunk driver. He was going over one hundred miles per hour when he rear-ended her, causing her car to roll and then flip end to end, stopping in a culvert. Passersby ignored her at first because it was right before Halloween, and they thought it was a Halloween prop. Knowing what my mom went through somehow wasn't enough to stop me from getting behind the wheel under the influence. The reason was that I was so depressed I didn't care. I thank God for caring about me and loving me when I didn't love myself. He cares for you too, no matter what mistakes you've made!

One of the most shameful days of my life turned into one of the biggest blessings. I was supposed to go to Coney Island with my best friend for her work's picnic day. We had this planned for quite some time, but guess what happened the night before? I went out and got drunker than I had ever gotten before. I spent the early morning hours throwing up in my bathtub while I let the hot water from the shower wash over me. I felt absolutely miserable, but I didn't want to let my friend down, so we still went. We weren't there long before I had to go to the bathroom to throw up some more. When she looked at me with deep disappointment in her eyes and said that she should just take me home, I felt like the worst friend and person on the planet. The drive home seemed to sober me up quickly and made me take a hard look at my life. This isn't the person I wanted to be. I knew I had to do better for my son, my friends, and family, and for myself. I decided right there to stop drinking, and honestly, it was easy for me. I had just a taste of the destruction that alcohol can cause, and I didn't want it to be the reason for any more brokenness in my life. I was done!

Once I gave up alcohol, I started going back to church and working on my relationship with the Lord. At this point, my son was about five years old. As my relationship with Christ grew, the depression and anger diminished. I stopped looking for a husband and a father for my son. I started focusing more and more attention on God and His Word. My mom always told me I needed to stop looking so hard for a husband and I guess she was right. It was only about six months after I stopped the search for a man, that I met the one God had for me all along.

Can you imagine all the heartaches we could avoid if we stopped striving so hard to get our own way and let God be God as we trust in His perfect timing?

I still had waves of depression that would try to creep into my life, but now that I was married, it was nothing like what I experienced during the six years of being a single mom. But then, around 2009, it hit me again, although in an entirely different way. It was something I was unfamiliar with. My second son was around a year old. All my dreams were coming true. He was an adorable and mostly happy baby. We moved to a new state that was only about a couple of hours away from family and we had settled in well. Outwardly, my life seemed wonderful. On the inside, however, I was fighting that demon called depression.

I did not know that you could get postpartum depression a full year after the baby is born, but apparently, that is what happened to me. I couldn't understand the horrible thoughts I was having. I felt like I didn't deserve to live. I thought I was a horrible, lazy mom, and that my family would be way better off without me. In my mind, I planned out how I was going to take my own life. ***I never googled anything to research the best ways to commit suicide. I didn't have to because Satan gave me the vision.*** I saw myself sneaking out of the house in the middle of the night, getting in my car, and driving down the street at a high speed until I found a good place with a lot of trees to crash into. I can still recall that scene in my mind as if it were a real place that I have visited many times.

Thankfully, I never followed through with that vision because when I went for my annual checkup, I just started weeping in the doctor's office. I was scared that they would try to take my children away, but they didn't. They recognized what I was dealing with and reassured me that everything was going to be okay. For a short time, I took medicine to help reset my mind. I don't really like taking medication, but I knew it was necessary for a little while.

Don't ever be afraid to reach out for help if you are depressed, especially if you are having thoughts of ending your life. Those thoughts are not from the Lord. You may wonder how God could even love you after all the things you've done or what's been done to you. I want to tell you what I told a young lady just today who told me those exact words.

> ***You are His child! He loves you regardless of what you've done.***

There's not a thing in this world that my boys could do that would make me love them any less than I do. Can you imagine how much greater God's love is for you? Matthew 7:11 says, "If you then, being evil, know how to give good gifts to your children, how much more will your Father who is in heaven give good things to those who ask Him!"

Although I was a Christian, I lived bound by fear, anxiety, and depression for way too many years. I thought that once I had the postpartum depression under control, that would be the end of the depression. But once again in 2015, anxiety hit me and deep depression soon followed. This was a tough year for me. It all started with issues with our neighbors; issues which I really didn't understand. We went from being the house where all the kids came to play, to the home where the children were no longer allowed to visit. Some of the deepest emotional pain I've ever felt came from the hurtful actions of my neighbors. These were people who I thought were my friends, but it's like everything turned sour overnight. I can't even explain what happened because I still don't understand it to this day.

In my heart, I really felt that I had done nothing wrong, but I suddenly found myself as the one everyone loved to hate. The worst part about it was watching our son stare out of his window, watching his friends play with each other. He couldn't understand why they could no longer play with him. Anxiety came over me like a rushing wave. I couldn't go outside anymore without feeling panicked. I always felt like the neighbors were talking about me. One of them had been a great sister in Christ and her son was my son's best friend. That was the one that hurt the most. I sat in my bed night after night sobbing as I asked the Lord to do something to change the situation. I was pregnant with our fourth son, so pregnancy hormones intensified everything that I was feeling.

In February 2015, I wrote in my journal, *"I can't focus. Fighting depression again. Isolating myself from the world. Don't want to cry anymore.*

Trying to think positive, but negative thoughts keep trying to consume me. Darkness. Sadness. Where is the light? I know it's right in front of me, but the darkness keeps blocking my view. Draw me out of this God! Once and for all! Guilt. Shame. Selfishness. Pain. Tears. Anger. Regret. Sadness. Alone. Tired."
I felt like my spirit had been completely crushed.

I would pray for God to change my neighbors' hearts toward me, and I asked Him to show me anything that I had done wrong. I prayed every day for my neighbors. Sometimes my prayers were for God to have vengeance on them because I was so angry, but usually, it was for God to bless them and save those who were lost. But no matter how I prayed, it didn't seem like anything was going to change.

I loved our home so much. On the inside, the house brought me so much joy. I loved everything about it. But every time I stepped outside, anxiety and fear crippled me. I find it fascinating how the anxiety happening with my home sort of paralleled my depression. The outward appearance of my life was fine, while inside I was having suicidal thoughts. My anxiety grew until I couldn't take it anymore and we put our home on the market. I couldn't believe that I was allowing other people to force me away from a home that I loved so much, but God knew I wouldn't move if I was comfortable.

> **Sometimes He allows us to go through painful situations because it's the only way He can get us to go where He wants to take us.**

Take the disciple John for example. Had he not been sentenced to life in prison on the island of Patmos, we might not have ever gotten the book of Revelation.

Our fourth son was born before our home sold. I had hoped to be moved before then, but it just didn't work out that way. His birth was by far the toughest for me. Not only did I have the least amount of support than any of my other births, but he ended up being my third and scariest emergency c-section. I wanted so badly to have a natural birth. I tried everything possible, like eating healthy, going to the chiropractor, and hiring a doula; but in the end, there was nothing I could do to prevent what happened. Once labor had begun, the baby and I were doing great until I was eight centimeters dilated.

I had labored for a very long time and had agreed to allow the doctor to break my water to get the show on the road. When she went to break my water, she couldn't get it to break, but blood started gushing out instead. Simultaneously, the baby's heart rate started dropping. I was so mad at myself for allowing them to intervene and I'll always wonder if they had ruptured something when they were trying to break my water. I was swiftly taken to the operating room to get the baby out as quickly as possible. I remember when they sat me up to put the epidural in my back, feeling a huge gush of blood leaving my body. I felt extremely weak and wondered if I would lose consciousness. There were several doctors and nurses in the room and the pace at which they were moving seemed to double after they confirmed what I had felt. I didn't know what was going on, but I sensed it was urgent. I was so scared, but all I could think to do was to pray for my baby. I wasn't even thinking about myself. I just wanted my baby to make it.

Later I found out that the very moment that the doctor took Gracen from my womb, the placenta had completely detached. If they hadn't moved as quickly as they did, we both could've died. Although I was extremely thankful for our lives, my heart felt crushed because that experience was a long way from the natural birth that I dreamed of and had fought so hard for.

Not getting the birth that I hoped for added to my already weakened emotional status. It took me an entire month to write anything in my journal that I had been writing in almost daily before Gracen was born. Partly because I was healing physically and had a newborn and a toddler in diapers, but also because I struggled to understand why God had allowed such suffering during the birth. I also grieved at the thought of not being able to have more children of my own. Pregnancy was now too dangerous to consider because of multiple complications and my uterus being paper thin. It's like the door was slammed shut on the thought of ever having a daughter of my own. It was all so very hard to process.

Finally, when I picked up the pen again, I wrote, *"God, I want to hand over all my pain and questions to You. I ask You for freedom and deliverance from the past, from all the hurt that I've gone through. I don't know why I'll never have a daughter from my womb. I don't understand all my surgeries and traumatic births. I don't understand the breastfeeding issues and pain or why Gracen has been so fussy. I don't understand the postpartum depression or issues with my neighbors. I don't understand why my husband has to suffer and deal with pain every single day. BUT I don't have to understand. I trust You that You are bigger than all of this and that we'll come out on the other side stronger than ever! Thank You for peace and hope of better things yet to come."*

I love that I've been journaling for so long. It helps me to see where my thoughts were and to recognize how far God has brought me. There I was dealing with so much grief and pain, but I can see the exact moment when faith rose within me as it spilled out onto the paper. If you don't journal, today is a great day to start writing in one.

Maybe you haven't experienced deep depression with suicidal thoughts, but you find yourself feeling down a lot. I've been there too. For me, the biggest reason I felt this way is comparison. I usually feel terrific about my life until I compare myself to others. One thing that gets to me most often is comparing my life with the moms who always seem to have everything together. You know, the ones whose houses are always spotless even if you pop in for a surprise visit. They're always fixing a nice meal for their family, keeping their children busy with activities, and seem so laid back even when their children are acting up. Just one visit to a house like that can send me in a downward spiral. I'll go home and either eat all the junk food I can get my hands on and mope around for the rest of the day or I'll get so angry at my life and start angry cleaning. Do you ever do that?

The two biggest motivations to get my house cleaned really fast are angry cleaning sessions and last-minute surprise company. Once I come back from my out-of-body experience that seems to happen during the angry cleaning, I question why I feel the way I do. Is a spotless house really that important to me? I sure hope not, because I can't even get my entire house clean, let alone keep it that way for more than ten minutes. If you're feeling down because you're comparing your life to someone else's, it's likely that you are envying something that God never intended for your own life. God called us to be a Mary, not a Martha. It's wonderful to have a spotless home, but if it comes at the cost of doing what God has specifically called you to do, you will chase your tail and waste your time and probably find yourself depressed.

Almost monthly I have to step back and take a hard look at my priorities in life. It's really the only way I can keep depression at bay. When I stay focused on what the Lord has called **me** to do, I am less likely to become jealous of someone else's life. If you're not sure where your priorities lie, then start with Biblical examples. Obviously, your very first priority should be the Lord Himself. The very first commandment is in Exodus 20:2-3, "I am the LORD your God, who brought you out of the land of Egypt, out of the house of bondage. You shall have no other gods before Me."

Is there something in your life that you have allowed to become your god? Recently I downloaded a seemingly innocent game on my phone. It didn't take long for me to get sucked into all the quests to earn rewards. It felt good helping my team members out by giving them lives and scoring points so that we could all reap the benefits. If you're in your twenties or younger, go ahead and call me cringey just like my sons do. You won't hurt my feelings. Anyway, it didn't take long to realize that this game quickly became a time suck and a distraction from the people and things that are truly important. It even became a reason that I didn't feel like getting to work on this book. If you're not careful, simple things like apps on your phone can derail you from fulfilling God's purpose for your life.

I want to also mention that too much screen time has been proven to lead to depression. Maybe it's because you're on social media where you mostly see the good parts of other people's lives. I know that if I'm not careful, seeing someone at the beach while I'm trapped in a cold climate can make me feel down. You can also fall into a routine of doing so much on your screens that you don't have time to accomplish the things that you know you need to do. This book isn't about how screens can negatively impact your life, but I know many people are struggling in this area and the phone has become an idol in their lives. Anything that you give more attention to than God is an idol.

Putting the Lord above everything else will help you figure out how you should really spend your time. I promise that when you do this, a transformation will happen. His voice will become clearer to you. He's there, wanting to show you the way, but you won't be able to hear from Him if you don't spend time with Him. It's hard to recognize the voice of someone that you won't take the time to listen to.

When was the last time you sat in stillness, allowing Him to speak to you? So often, people think that there must be a revival fire type of church service to hear from God and they forget it was not in the earthquake or the fire that the LORD was found, but in a still small voice. (See I Kings 19:11-12.)

SUICIDAL THOUGHTS

I can't end this chapter without speaking directly to those of you who have battled suicidal thoughts. Maybe you're there right now. Perhaps you've already written a goodbye letter and have planned out how you're going to take action. I can only imagine the pain that you have endured to reach such desperation.

I've asked the Holy Spirit to give me the right words for you and this is what I hear:

Don't you ever give up! You are loved and wanted! Your life matters!

Satan is a liar, and his plan is to stop you from advancing in the purposes and plans that the Lord has for your life. You may not think that you can go on living even one more day, but if you keep hanging on, He will not only provide a better way out, but He can use you as a light to guide others out of the same darkness that you have been experiencing. This isn't just something I am making up to make you feel better. The Word of God confirms it in II Corinthians 1:3-4, It says,

> *Blessed be the God and Father of our Lord Jesus Christ, the Father of mercies and God of all comfort, who comforts us in all our tribulation, that we may be able to comfort those who are in any trouble, with the comfort with which we ourselves are comforted by God.*

I know that it's difficult to see a light at the end of the tunnel when you are surrounded by darkness. I think back to the book of Job in the Bible. Job went through more suffering than anyone I know, and I have met people who have lived pretty devastating lives. But think about what would've happened if Job had ended his own life. He would have aborted God's plan to restore his life by giving him double of everything that he had before. (Job 42:10) I pray that hope fills your heart today; hope that your future will be better than your past and that the Lord will restore back everything that's been stolen from you, double!

PRAYER FOR THOSE WHO ARE DEPRESSED

If you are reading this right now, then know that I have prophesied into this very moment just for you. Wherever you are, this prayer is for you! I'm going to write this out as if you are the one saying it. I pray that as you speak it out loud, the power of God will hit you and destroy every work of the enemy.

Father God, I come to you right now in the name of Jesus. I ask You to show Yourself to me in a powerful and mighty way. I pray for a shift in the atmosphere and in my heart. Holy Spirit, fill me until I overflow into the lives of others who need a breakthrough. Drown out the voices of the enemy! Reveal to me Your divine plan to rescue me from the darkness that I have been experiencing. Your Word says that You have delivered us, so I hold fast to the words of Colossians 1:13-14, *"He has delivered us from the power of darkness and conveyed us into the kingdom of the Son of His love, in whom we have redemption through His blood, the forgiveness of sins."* Thank You for the blood that was shed for me and for forgiving me of every sin, no matter how great or how small!

Lord, set a new fire in my soul that will propel me toward the abundant life that You died to give me. I pray for freedom and deliverance to happen right now! Freedom from every tormenting spirit, in the name of Jesus! Depression and oppression, you have no place! You must go right now! Suicidal thoughts… you are no longer allowed. You have been found out as a lie from Satan. Go back to the pit of hell where you belong!

I pray for restoration of everything the enemy has stolen in every area of my life. Heal every physical and emotional scar. Renew my mind right now with the mind of Christ. I speak restoration of joy and peace; that the thoughts that have been haunting me will cease right now in the name of Jesus and that You will put a wall up around my mind that the enemy can no longer penetrate. Guard my heart and my mind from this moment forward. Help me to always remember who I am in Christ. I am strong, more than a conqueror! I pray God that you will reveal my next steps and help me pursue a godly life with a fresh anointing. Let me feel Your presence right now as the weight that I've been carrying is being lifted. In Jesus's name I pray, Amen!

REFLECT

Are you dealing with a painful situation that you just can't make sense of? Or maybe it's something that has happened in your life that you just can't seem to let go of. Could it be that God has allowed your circumstances because He knows that it's the only way to bring a big change in your life? I want to encourage you to get out your journal or start a new one right now and pour out your heart to the Lord. Use your computer if you don't enjoy writing on paper.

If you allow writing to become a habit as you keep seeking the Lord for help, you will see just as I did, when your doubts and fears shift into belief and faith. Spend some time in silence and write what you feel you're hearing from Him. His voice is the most important one of all and it's such a treasure to have written reminders of what He has spoken to you.

If you're not sure what to write, perhaps the prayer you just prayed touched your life. If so, then write about it. It's moments like that you'll never want to forget. It will become a cherished gift in your life as you mark exactly when God brought you out of the darkness and into His glorious light.

My Reflections

CHAPTER NINE

FROM FEAR TO VICTORY

There are endless examples of fear in the Bible. Fear goes all the way back to the very first humans who hid from God in the garden. There are also many accounts of people in the Bible who encountered anxiety and depression. Job, Jonah, and David are the first few that come to my mind. There is much to be learned from these stories and often we just read through them without giving them much thought. I want to share just a couple of stories and the revelations that God gave me as I searched the scriptures for verses to be used in this book.

At the beginning of Judges, chapter 7, Gideon was about to go up against the Midianites in battle. God told Gideon that there were too many men in his army which would cause them to believe that they won the battle through their own efforts. God spoke to Gideon in verse 3 and told him to tell the people that *"whoever is fearful and afraid, let him turn and depart at once from Gilead."* A whopping twenty-two thousand people left because they were fearful! The Lord continued to weed out the people (almost ten thousand more) until there were just three hundred men left in Gideon's army. God then used those three hundred men, armed only with trumpets, empty pitchers, and torches inside the pitchers, to conquer the Midianites.

In this story, God only used those who weren't fearful! **What if you're missing out on the fullness of God's plans for your life**

because He knows you are fearful? I refuse to be that person any longer. I will charge forward at full speed saying, "Here I am Lord. Use me!" I don't care anymore what anyone else thinks of my capabilities. I don't care about other people's opinions. I will not be nervous as I tread uncharted waters. I trust God has GREAT BIG PLANS for me, and I can't take for granted the time that I have left here on earth. Are you ready to make those same declarations? I pray for a stirring in your heart right now; a boldness rising in your spirit. I pray for ALL fear to be removed so that God can see that you are ready to move forward just like those three hundred men in Gideon's army.

Let's look at another story. Most people think of the prophet Elijah as a great man of God who couldn't possibly be fearful. He's the one who commanded the rain to cease for three and a half years and the one who called fire down from heaven. He prophesied that Ahab's sons would all be destroyed, that Jezebel would be eaten by dogs, and that Ahaziah would die from his illness. At Elijah's word, kings trembled, the rain stopped and then started again, fire fell, a jug of oil didn't run dry, a boy was raised from the dead, revival broke out, and idolatrous false prophets were killed.

There is a specific event in Elijah's life that happened in I Kings 18:20-40 where the focus is usually on the miracle that took place, but the story after the miracle is rarely told. Although I've read through the Bible a few times, it wasn't until our pastor preached on this story, that I realized there was so much more beyond the miracle that took place. I'm talking about where Elijah came against 450 false prophets, better known as the prophets of Baal. Elijah challenged the false prophets to call on the name of their god and he would call on the name of his God and whichever one made fire fall on the altar, that one would be the One True God.

In case you aren't familiar with this story, the prophets of Baal could not cause fire to come, no matter how hard they tried. But when it was Elijah's turn, before calling on the name of God, he drenched the wood and the offering with so much water that it ran around the altar and filled up the trench. The Lord answered Elijah by causing fire to fall, consuming all the burnt offering, the wood, and all the water that had been poured out. The people who were gathered around and witnessed what had happened fell on their faces and said that the Lord is God. Then Elijah told the people to seize the false prophets and not let any of them escape. Elijah then took them to the brook Kishon and slaughtered them.

I try to put myself in Elijah's shoes. What faith it had to take to stand before all those men and believe that God would cause fire to fall! Most of us today have trouble believing God for small miracles, like taking away back pain or getting a promotion. I've witnessed several miracles in my own life and each one has caused an increase in my faith. As my faith continued to grow, anxiety and fear decreased more and more. I try to imagine asking God to cause fire to fall right in front of me and Him answering by making it happen. Would that be enough to cause me to never be fearful again? You would think so! But here's the rest of Elijah's story that rarely gets told.

After Elijah had performed many miracles and witnessed fire falling on the altar, he received a message from Queen Jezebel that said that she promised to do the exact same thing to him as he had done to the prophets of Baal (remember, he slaughtered them). Instead of standing in faith, fear immediately set in, causing Elijah to run for his life. He ran for an entire day until he reached the wilderness, and it was there that he asked God to end his life. This shows us that no one is immune to fear or exempt from depression and suicidal thoughts!

Elijah never doubted God's power, because he had seen firsthand the works of the Lord. What he doubted was God's plan for his future. Elijah's heart was troubled because he thought he was the only true prophet left, but in I Kings 19:15-18, The Lord revealed His plans to Elijah and told him that there were still seven thousand in Israel who had not bowed down to Baal. It was in those verses that hope was restored for Elijah.

What about you? Are you doubting God's plans for your future? Has life gotten you so down that you've cried out for God to just end it? I encourage you to not give up hope because God can use one gentle whisper to change everything. Like I mentioned in the previous chapter, you may be waiting for God to move in a mighty, powerful way, but He may come like He did to Elijah in a still small voice. Don't miss it!

> *Then He said, "Go out, and stand on the mountain before the LORD." And behold, the LORD passed by, and a great and strong wind tore into the mountains and broke the rocks in pieces before the LORD, but the LORD was not in the wind; and after the wind an earthquake; but the LORD was not in the earthquake; and after the earthquake a fire, but the LORD was not in the fire; and after the fire a still small voice. I Kings 19:11-12*

These stories have touched a little on fear and depression, but what about anxiety? David had a multitude of anxieties from which the Lord comforted him (Psalm 94:19). Job had anxious thoughts because of the turmoil within him (Job 20:2). While the Bible doesn't always call it anxiety, we know it was indeed anxiety that caused many Bible icons to have fearful responses. For example, Peter began to sink into the water as he became fearful/anxious. Martha was full of anxiety as she worried about being the perfect host. Martha also showed anxiety when her brother Lazarus had passed away and she was upset with Jesus for not getting to him sooner. There are countless other events in the Bible that involve fear, anxiety, and depression. You could turn to just about any book in the Bible and find something on one of these topics. I encourage you to search the scriptures for these topics to discover stories that speak to you in a personal way.

There is just too much goodness and hope to be found in the Bible to allow yourself to remain where you are right now. His Word is as true today as it was when Jesus was walking this earth. It's time that we stop thinking that miracles aren't for today or that they only happen to other people. It's time to stand firm on what the Bible says and not accept no for an answer. Keep believing until you see healing come, until you see salvation for your loved ones, or whatever else it is you are believing for.

Some people may argue that sometimes God answers with a no. Personally, I'm at a place in life where I'll keep believing for whatever I need from Him, even if His final answer ends up being a no, I know He hears me. He knows my heart and I know I am His daughter whom He loves more than I could ever imagine. Even if I never see my desires come to pass, I know that He's still a good God and I trust that His plans for my life are far better than what I could do without Him. He sees the entire picture, whereas I only get a glimpse. Let me share with you just how I got to this level of faith. It's something that just recently happened.

THE SCARIEST THING I'VE EVER TOLD THE LORD

The Lord speaks to me almost every single night in my dreams. It's such a gift! Usually, the dreams give me little hints about what will happen in my future, or they will expand on things that are happening in my life right now. Occasionally He gives me dreams that are meant for other people. I love when He does that because I love speaking into other people's lives.

A couple of weeks ago my dreams shifted, and I began having dark dreams that had symbols like tornados, car wrecks, and heart attacks. As I prayed for revelation, the Lord told me that Satan is coming against me and my family. I immediately went into spiritual warfare mode and began commanding Satan to take his hands off my family. I used Bible verses like Isaiah 54:17 to war against Satan, where I would say, "No weapon formed against me or my family will prosper, in Jesus's name."

Night after night, the dark dreams were still happening regardless of how hard I prayed or how much I commanded Satan to leave me alone. I told God the scariest thing I've ever said to Him in my life. I said, *"Lord, I give it ALL to you. This battle is Yours! I know that You already have the victory. You know my future. I trust Your plans, God. Even if something tragic happens, I trust You allowed it for a purpose and that You will get glory even through the toughest circumstances... I'm ready Lord."* I told God that I was ready for whatever He wanted to do, and I meant it. Even if it would come in a way that looked like a complete disaster, I would accept it because I know He will work everything out for good.

After having this conversation with the Lord, the nightmares immediately stopped. I believe He was waiting on me to *fully* trust Him. Those were the scariest words I've ever committed to the Lord, but the results were even more peace than I had before. Regardless of what life throws my way, I know I can deal with it because I've already given it to Him to handle.

Honestly, in just the two weeks since then, I have faced immense trials. My aunt died suddenly in a tragic car accident, my mom spent three days in the hospital for what we first thought was her heart, another one of my aunts was thrown off her horse because the reins broke leaving her with two broken ribs and stitches in her head, and I have been dealing with a very odd pain in my stomach among other unpleasant symptoms. Through all of this, I know God had prepared me, and because I've stood firm and trusted Him, I can see His glory in every situation that has happened.

My aunt who passed away was one of twelve siblings and she was one of the few that I know was saved. I've never had as much peace at a funeral as I did at hers; partially because I know she's with Jesus, but also because I'm not at the same place spiritually as I was five or ten years ago. So much growth has happened in my life over just the past few years. I can truly celebrate now when I know that my loved one is with Jesus. As for my mom, even though an EKG showed something wrong with her heart, all the tests that were done in the hospital revealed that her heart is fine. My aunt who was thrown from the horse is going to recover, and my stomach stopped hurting after a few days.

As I was almost ready to publish this book, I learned more about my aunt who was thrown from her horse, and I just had to come back and add in the rest of her story. During her hospital stay, she had scans on her back and lungs which revealed the broken ribs. What we didn't know right away is that those scans also showed that a nodule in her right lung. When she followed up with her family doctor to remove the stitches from her head, he sent her to have more tests. After some testing and a breast biopsy, they diagnosed her with metastatic breast cancer. Although this was devastating news, we believe that the cancer would have gone undetected if it weren't for her getting thrown from the horse. Prior to her accident, she had no lumps or pain, or anything else that had been concerning. She also had mammograms every year for twenty-five years and nothing ever showed up. Her last yearly mammogram was not even a month prior to the diagnosis, and it was completely clear. Here's an even crazier part of her story; she went back to the barn a couple of weeks after being released from the hospital and when she examined her horse's reins, they were completely intact! Even though cancer is a diagnosis that no one wants to hear, I thank God that He made it known so she could start getting the proper treatment. I choose to walk in faith and believe that God has completely healed her body.

Daily the Lord is increasing my faith as I continue to trust His plans regardless of what my circumstances look like. Do you know what faith really is? The Bible tells us exactly what it is in *Hebrews 11:1*. *"Now faith is the substance of things hoped for, the evidence of things not seen."* What does that mean? It means that even though my oldest son isn't going to church, I believe with all my heart that God is bringing him back. I don't walk around worried that my son won't make it to heaven. I stand on God's Word and declare my son's salvation. The Word is in him, and the Holy Spirit is guiding him closer to the Lord every day.

Faith means that even though I felt pain in my stomach, I believed God had already healed me. Another scripture I stand on for healing that goes right along with Hebrews 11:1 is II Corinthians 5:7, *"For we walk by faith, not by sight."* Even though I may *see* evidence of being sick, I *choose* to believe that I am healed. Faith means that I believe with all my heart that I'm not writing this book in vain. Even though I'm still working out all the details, I believe it will be a tool that will set thousands of people free. And yes, I'm believing that it will be a top seller that will be a huge financial blessing to our family. Faith is looking at your current situation no matter how it seems and declaring that there is more!

There is one thing that stands in your way of having a greater level of faith, and that obstacle is called doubt. Faith and doubt cannot coexist. That's why when He builds your faith, you absolutely will notice doubt decreasing. You can't increase your faith while you hold on to doubt.

I want you to get real for a minute and ask yourself if you doubt Jesus will really set you free of the things that have been holding you back. Because remember what I just told you? **You cannot increase your faith while holding onto doubt.**

Before we move on to the next chapter, I want to leave you with some powerful scriptures that are not meant to condemn you, but rather help build your faith as you see how much doubt is part of the enemy's plan for your life, and what can happen when doubt is removed. Meditate on these scriptures and maybe write out a few that really speak to you.

> *But let him ask in faith, with no doubting, for he who doubts is like a wave of the sea driven and tossed by the wind. James 1:6*

> *For assuredly, I say to you, whoever says to this mountain, 'Be removed and be cast into the sea,' and does not doubt in his heart, but believes that those things he says will be done, he will have whatever he says. Mark 11:23*

> *Trust in the LORD with all your heart, and lean not on your own understanding. Proverbs 3:5*

> *And whatever things you ask in prayer, believing, you will receive. Matthew 21:22*

> *May the God of hope fill you with all joy and peace in believing [through the experience of your faith] that by the power of the Holy Spirit you will abound in hope and overflow with confidence in His promises. Romans 15:13 (AMP)*

> *But without faith it is impossible to please Him, for he who comes to God must believe that He is, and that He is a rewarder of those who diligently seek Him. Hebrews 11:6*

> *My brethren, count it all joy when you fall into various trials, knowing that the testing of your faith produces patience. James 1:2*

> *In this you greatly rejoice, though now for a little while, if need be, you have been grieved by various trials, that the genuineness of your faith, being much more precious than gold that perishes, though it is tested by fire, may be found to praise, honor, and glory at the revelation of Jesus Christ, whom having not seen you love. Though now you do not see Him, yet believing, you rejoice with joy inexpressible and full of glory, receiving the end of your faith—the salvation of your souls. I Peter 1:6-9*

> *Watch, stand fast in the faith, be brave, be strong. I Corinthians 16:13*

> *For whatever is born of God overcomes the world. And this is the victory that has overcome the world—our faith. I John 5:4*

> *By faith we understand that the worlds were framed by the word of God, so that the things which are seen were not made of the things which are visible. Hebrews 11:3*

> *By faith Abel offered to God a more excellent sacrifice than Cain, through which he obtained witness that he was righteous, God testifying of his gifts; and through it he being dead still speaks. Hebrews 11:4*

> *By faith Enoch was taken away so that he did not see death, 'and was not found, because God had taken him'; for before he was taken he had this testimony, that he pleased God. Hebrews 11:5*

> *By faith Noah, being divinely warned of things not yet seen, moved with godly fear, prepared an ark for the saving of his household, by which he condemned the world and became heir of the righteousness which is according to faith. Hebrews 11:7*

> *By faith Abraham obeyed when he was called to go out to the place which he would receive as an inheritance. Hebrews 11:8*

> *By faith Sarah herself also received strength to conceive seed, and she bore a child when she was past the age, because she judged Him faithful who had promised. Hebrews 11:11*

REFLECT

If you were to continue on the same path that you are currently on, what would your future look like in five or ten more years? Seriously stop and try to picture it.

I know that for many of you, you don't have to stop and try to picture anything because you've been living a life that has been going around the same mountain for years. You feel like nothing will ever change because no matter how hard you've tried, everything has stayed the same. I completely understand where you're coming from and that is why I'm praying and believing that *something* from this book will be the key to your breakthrough.

Are you truly desperate for your freedom? Remember back in chapter two of this book where I mentioned giving the Lord everything? Did you do it, or did you just skip on through so you could keep reading? If you didn't do it, then I dare you to get alone with God right now and tell Him you are ready to give Him EVERYTHING! Stop holding on to parts of your life that you think you have control of. Tell Him you are ready for whatever He has for your life. But you can't just say it, you have to mean it! When you give Him a *complete* yes, I guarantee things will shift for you. There will be new opportunities that might make your heart pound and you will be terrified to step out and do it, but if it's where the Lord is leading you, you have to go for it! Making this decision could change the entire course of your life. You will finally see yourself getting farther and farther away from that mountain that you've been circling all these years. When you put your entire life in His hands, He's not going to just leave you there with nothing. The first thing He'll probably give you is a sense of peace like you've never experienced before.

Imagine yourself carrying around a backpack that is weighted down with all the worries and cares of this world. You may have some doubt, anger, anxiety, or depression in there too. You've been lugging this thing around for as long as you can remember. You've gotten really used to it, so sometimes you don't even realize how much it's weighing you down and keeping you from moving forward in life, but it's extremely heavy! When you finally trust God enough to say, "I give it ALL to You.", then at that very moment, the backpack is emptied, and you immediately feel lighter.

When I did this, it felt terrifying and exhilarating at the same time, but it was yet another turning point for me, another piece of my story from fear to victory. I believe your story isn't over, but it's only just beginning. I pray that as you let go of all that has been holding you back, you will see victory after victory unfold in your life.

My Reflections

CHAPTER TEN

WHAT FREEDOM LOOKS LIKE

What does freedom from fear, anxiety, and depression really look like? I'm going to be honest with you and let you know that every now and then those demons try to rear their ugly heads. On the bright side though, I now recognize the attacks much quicker than I ever did before, and the fear doesn't have enough time to fully invade my thoughts. Because you are reading this book, I can assume that you've been through some tough times. But here's a huge key that you need to keep in mind when darkness comes. You've been through this before and you survived! When terrible thoughts try to take over your mind, remember that you've dealt with this before, and no matter how scared you feel, tell yourself that you will be okay.

When I wake up with some crazy pain in the middle of the night, my mind still wants to jump immediately to the worst-case scenario, but I'm able to talk myself down before it gets out of control and turns into a full-blown panic attack. In fact, this just happened to me this week.

I woke up with pain in my left shoulder blade. It was an odd type of pain, unlike the typical aches and pains that I often experience. Most people wouldn't think much of it, but I know that the signs of a heart attack in women can be very subtle, and I remember reading about shoulder pain being one of the signs. I went to Google to research the signs of a heart attack in women. Remember me telling you earlier not to do that? Yeah, I still do it sometimes. But, within minutes, I started telling myself, "No! I'm not having a heart attack." I opened my Bible app and started reading the Bible. There is nothing that will calm you down quite like reading the Word of God. I laid in bed reading for over an hour before I was able to relax enough to put the phone down and go back to sleep. When I woke up in the morning, my body was perfectly fine.

There was another incident that happened during the writing of this book. Once again, I abruptly woke up in the middle of the night and my chest was hurting badly. I couldn't take a full breath because every time I tried to breathe in, the pain just wouldn't allow it. My heart was racing, and I had pain in my left shoulder blade. Aaron rubbed my back as we both prayed, and I tried my best to calm down. I knew in my heart that it was just gas because I had been hiccupping and burping, but it can be very terrifying dealing with chest pain and not being able to breathe properly. As I paced back and forth, I walked in my bathroom where I saw my reflection in the mirror. Immediately I recognized the spirit of fear that had come upon me. As soon as I realized it, I stood tall and commanded the spirit of fear to go in the name of Jesus. I made the decision that I wasn't reverting to my old ways. In an instant, all pain was gone, and I felt such peace come over me. I knew the Lord had touched my body because of the immediate change and because I didn't hiccup or burp a single time after that.

Have you ever seen the TV show Ordinary Joe? It plays out three different scenarios of Joe's life. It shows you what his life would be like now, based on the big decisions he made after college. That show got me thinking about how differently my life would be right now if fear, anxiety, and depression were never a part of my past. Where would I be now? I highly doubt it would be right where I am now, but then I wouldn't have written this book for you.

But where would I be? Outside of becoming a mother, my biggest dream in life was to become a famous country singer. I gave up on that dream shortly after my first son was born; after all, he was one of my biggest dreams that came true. But was becoming a mother really my excuse for closing the door on other dreams, or was it fear? Would I have continued putting myself out there, trying to make it in the music industry if I wasn't afraid? To be honest, all those what-ifs played out in my mind then just as they did when I was offered that trip to Playa Del Carmen, Mexico. What if I couldn't make it and I lost our home? What if focusing on music took too much time away from my son? What if I did make it? I'd have to travel a lot, and I was afraid to fly! Could it be that if I had pressed through all those fears, that I would've made it big time and you would be paying for one of my concert tickets instead of paying for my book?

Another thing I'll always wonder is if I would have had more children if fear weren't a factor. Would I have been able to have my own baby girl? In my heart, I know that the answer to those questions is yes because God gave me a very vivid vision a long time ago after the birth of our last son. He showed me all my boys standing out in a field and there were many other children next to them, but they looked like shadows. I could tell that some were girls because of the shadows of their hair and the dresses they were wearing. I knew He was showing me I would've had many more children if it weren't for fear. At this point in my life, I'm past that desire to have more babies of my own, so it's not really fear keeping us from having more now. Our boys are currently ages seven to twenty-three, so I'm ready for life beyond babies and eventually, I'll look forward to grandbabies.

Just as you can't live a life of what-ifs as you face new decisions, you also cannot allow the what-ifs of the past to continue to haunt your thoughts. I have had to let go of wondering how different my life may be now if I had made other choices along the way. Dwelling on the past changes nothing! If you've read through this book and have taken time to reflect on each chapter, then you have thought about your fears, faced them head on, discovered where Jesus was as you were going through the trials, and you've figured out the root of all your fears. Now it's time to move forward. It's time for a brand-new beginning, starting right where you are.

If I could save just one person from living a life bound by fear, anxiety, and depression, then this entire book was worth every second of discipline and time away from my family that it took to write it.

Back in chapter seven I shared with you how I thought my life might be different if it weren't for fear. Now that I'm on the other side of it all, I can honestly say that it looks like what I thought it would, but even so much more.

It really looks like:

- Spending most of my summers outside, soaking up the sunshine. I still don't like bees and wasps, but I can calmly move away from them now instead of freaking out and running away screaming.
- Exploring many new places. I recently took my first ever trip where it was just me and my friend. I could trust God and my husband with our boys at home while I was away. I also go hiking a lot with my boys. That can be a scary experience as you consider snakes and other dangers, but so far, it's been nothing short of amazing.
- Allowing our children to ride with other people.
- Having complete peace when there is a threat of severe weather and even amid the storms.
- Going to church year-round, even when flu and Covid were at extremely high numbers. I don't just attend church, but I happily hug everyone I can, and I consider it an honor to lay hands on the sick and pray for them.

- Not watching the news! Honestly, all that does is add fuel to your fears. And for many of you, social media can be worse than the news.
- Being happy for others when they get something I didn't…like a natural birth experience.
- Not freaking out every time I get a strange pain, or at least being able to put a stop to it more quickly.
- Freedom! Freedom from other people's opinions and trying to please them. Freedom from the fear of failure, and instead, being able to focus on what the Lord has called me to do.
- Happiness abounds! People who knew me before, and know me now, just can't get over the drastic change in my demeanor.
- My house stays cleaner because I have more energy and I have been able to develop good routines for our family. Keeping a clean house was almost impossible when I dealt with depression.
- Stepping into my callings. I love praying for others and speaking life and truth into their situations.
- Writing this book and being an encouragement to so many others. My friends come to me now because they know I understand what they are going through. I've said this many times but it's worth repeating: God wants you healed too so that you can be the one ministering to others.
- My dream life has increased significantly. I used to remember a couple of dreams per week, but now the Lord speaks to me in dreams, and I average remembering three to five dreams every single night.
- Being able to truly relax and trust God. No more striving to do things my own way.

> Supernatural peace! I honestly believe that whatever happens, good or bad, the Lord is in control. He is not surprised by any of it, so why should I be?

LIFE WITHOUT FEAR DURING A GLOBAL PANDEMIC

I am so incredibly thankful that God freed me before the height of the coronavirus pandemic. If He hadn't done that for me, I imagine that I would have visited the ER at least another time or two. This part of the book will not be comfortable for some people, but I want to be completely transparent. I want you to know that I have lived through the last few years absolutely unafraid! My husband and I have had Covid at least once, possibly twice, and I have lost a loved one around my age because of Covid and know many others who have had to walk through the same tragic path. I understand just how real the virus is, but fear or anxiety did not overtake me because of it. I have not once felt like I needed a mask or a vaccine to protect me, because I have had complete trust in the Lord. I don't even fear going to pray for someone who is sick and possibly has Covid. I stay prayed up and believe with all my heart that Jesus still wants us to mimic Him. He went straight to the lepers and laid His hands on them. Why should we do things differently? I John 2:6 says, "He who says he abides in Him ought himself also walk just as He walked."

For God to take someone like me, who was terrified to take her children to church during flu season and bring such deliverance that I have walked through a global pandemic fearlessly, should show you just how mighty our miracle-working God is. The transformation has been so life-changing that it just can't be explained naturally.

COMPARING THE OLD AND THE NEW LIFE

Just yesterday I was talking to a friend who has known me for over ten years. We were comparing the old me with the new me. She recalled how even though I'm older now, ten years ago I appeared to be in my forties, and now I look like I'm in my twenties. I hear that from many people. I love watching their jaws drop when I tell them I have a twenty-three-year-old son. My friend also commented that I used to have facial wrinkles that no longer exist and that my hair is fuller and much more beautiful now. She even said that my face used to have a gray tone to it, and I always seemed so sad. Well, that's because I usually was. We compared current pictures to those that were taken several years ago, and I was amazed to see the difference in my skin tone for myself. I have also just realized that my skin is tighter. I have literally cried because of the bags under my eyes, but I recently noticed that those bags are practically gone. I truly think that so many of my skin issues were caused by years of worry and sadness.

When I reflect on my behavior prior to being set free from bondage, it breaks my heart. Are there people in your life that you try to avoid because they have a way of sucking the life out of you? I was that person. It's no wonder people avoided my phone calls. Something that you may be surprised to know (or maybe not because you have the same issue) is that I dreaded Sundays. It never seemed to fail that while we were getting ready for church, something always went wrong. Much of the time it was all because of my own horrible attitude. I didn't feel like getting out of bed. Then I wasn't happy about how I looked, or I couldn't find the right clothes to wear. If it wasn't me, then you could count on at least one kid having issues that caused frustration every single Sunday. Because of the chaos while getting ready for church, my husband and I would argue in the car, and then we struggled to enjoy the service.

I used to sit in church with anger permeating the depths of my soul. I truly didn't want to be there, and frequently, I got up in the middle of service to find a place to hide, like in the bathroom or the foyer. The times that I stayed for service, I felt as if I had a straitjacket on my body during worship, keeping my hands from being lifted toward heaven, and duct tape on my mouth preventing me from giving the Lord praise with my lips. Satan didn't want the Lord to have my worship.

God later revealed to me that the spirit of oppression was operating in my life. If you feel you just can't break through to where you can enjoy life again, then you may have that same spirit keeping you bound. It is just like any other evil force and God has given you the authority to make it leave. Every name must bow to God Almighty. Command it to go right now in Jesus's name!

Now let's talk about the new me! I think the best way to describe myself is that I have lived the last few years bursting at the seams with the light of Jesus. I just can't help but be happy most of the time. There is a new level of boldness and confidence that I carry. One of my very respected friends described the new me as having Holy boldness. I just love that! I dream of speaking to thousands of people at conferences where my testimony will help set them free. I believe with all my heart that this dream will become a reality as I keep moving forward, knowing that people need to hear my testimony. I am no longer timid because I trust what II Timothy 1:7 says. He has given me POWER!

Now I absolutely understand who I am. I am who God says I am and anything that doesn't line up with that is a lie. I used to have very low self-esteem, but now I know I was created for God's glory, and He didn't make any mistakes in making me (or you). I'm also way more outgoing! The old me used every excuse to stay home, but the new me thrives on adventuring out into the world. My husband and teenage son are into magnet fishing and metal detecting, and I have enjoyed all the new places we've discovered as we've tried to find areas to do those things.

Relinquishing fear, anxiety, and depression has completely changed my countenance and my outlook on life. I'm dreaming and hoping again, believing that God has a glorious future for me. I'm also in the best physical shape that I've been in for many years and have had very few health issues. Almost everything that has come against me was just a test of my faith, but with His help, I was able to overcome it all. There honestly aren't enough words to describe how much I have been transformed, but I assure you that, had I known what freedom was truly like, I would've fought a lot harder to get here sooner!

REFLECT

What is one step you can take today to live a life without fear? For some, that may look like just getting out of the house. For others, maybe it will be turning the TV off or getting off Facebook and opening your Bible, allowing God's Word to speak truth to your soul. Maybe you will vow to stop googling things you know will lead to more anxious thoughts. Or maybe it's time to call your doctor to schedule blood work just to make sure everything looks great. Pick just one simple thing to do today.

Whatever you choose to do, you need to understand that fear, anxiety, and depression are the plans of the enemy. We must fight for our victory, and we must be battle ready at all times. Ephesians chapter six shows you exactly how to put on the full armor of God. And when you've done all that you know to do, just keep standing. Stand on God's Word! He is faithful to those who put their trust in Him.

My Reflections

CHAPTER ELEVEN

THE KEYS TO HEALING AND DELIVERANCE

I wrote these keys to your freedom in no particular order because it all depends on exactly what you are currently dealing with. It's very personal because there is no one-size-fits-all solution. As you read through each of these keys, there will probably be certain topics that your eyes are drawn to. If you have come here with an open heart and a genuine desire to seek freedom, I believe the Holy Spirit will guide you right to the areas that you need to prioritize.

Key #1 Forgiveness

A huge key in the healing process for me was to forgive everyone who has ever hurt me. If you are harboring any unforgiveness in your heart, you are leaving a door wide open for Satan to continue having influence over your life. Paul says in II Corinthians 2:10-11, "Now whom you forgive anything, I also forgive. For if indeed I have forgiven anything, I have forgiven that one for your sakes in the presence of Christ, lest Satan should take advantage of us; for we are not ignorant of his devices." To "take advantage of" means to profit from a situation. If you are not careful to forgive those who have brought an offense, Satan can step in and use that against you.

Unforgiveness allows Satan to take what is rightfully yours. He can steal your peace, joy, hope, restoration, and a million other things, just because you choose to continue to hold on to the hurt and pain that someone else has caused. You must forgive! There are no excuses for unforgiveness in the Bible. The longer you hold on to it, the longer you will suffer.

I have forgiven my dad for the pain and suffering he caused my family. I want to add that one of my greatest desires growing up was to have my dad sitting with us in church. Every time I went to church with my mom or my grandmother, I would look around and see other little girls with their daddies. It always made me incredibly sad, but I never stopped praying for my dad's salvation. I want you to know that he gave his life to Christ at the age of sixty-five. So, if you're still believing for the salvation of a loved one, if they are breathing, there is hope.

I have also forgiven the boy who raped me and every man since then who has caused any type of hurt in my life. I forgave my oldest son's biological dad for not being a father to my son. I forgave him for abandonment and lies that were told. I'm so thankful that my husband stepped in and filled shoes he didn't have to. He has treated Gavin like his very own from day one. He is the most selfless, faithful man I know, and I am truly blessed to be his wife. He has loved and respected me in a way that no other man has ever done, so I finally believe that all men are not created equally. I hope our sons will love their future spouses with the same kind of love that Aaron has given me.

I forgave the neighbors who caused me to move from a home that I loved. Remember how I said that the one neighbor that hurt me the most was a fellow sister in Christ? Well, within the first year of moving to our new home, we also changed churches. We started going to a small, but awesome and growing church.

Wouldn't you know it? After only attending that church for a few months, I heard a familiar voice directly behind me during praise and worship. It was my old neighbor! I asked the Lord what to do. I had to fight the feeling of panic. I heard a strong voice telling me to ask her to forgive me. At that point, I started having arguments in my mind with the Lord because I didn't think that I had done anything wrong. I knew once the music stopped, Pastor Brent would ask us to turn around and greet those around us. My heart was beating so strongly that I felt like it was going to leap out of my chest, and I could feel the heat in my cheeks. I kept hearing God say, "Ask her to forgive you!" I don't remember exactly how the conversation went, but I hugged her and asked her to forgive me, and she immediately said that she did. It was awkward for me for a while, but eventually, we became great friends again, and even better, our sons are once again best friends.

The Lord has shown me you can run and hide from someone all you want to because of offense, but if He wants that person to be in your life, He will make a way. And if you are obedient in how you handle the reunification, it could become one of your greatest blessings.

Key #2 Change your expectations

As I forgave my brothers, my parents, and many others for the hurt they caused because of various situations over the years, God showed me that much of the pain that I had experienced was because of my own expectations. There have been many times that I expected more out of others than they were willing or able to give.

I have also had to come to terms with the fact that we are all so different. I can't expect others to be the same as me. Expecting others to be like you could be the spark that ignites a whole flame of bitterness, anger, sadness, or depression. For example, I'm an encourager. There's not a single day that goes by that I don't reach out to someone with a word of encouragement. If I'm not careful, I can fall into a downward spiral quickly when no one is reaching out to me, and that small flame of sadness turns into a wildfire that is hard to put out. This has been a huge area of growth in my life and the Lord has shown me I can't take it personally because my gifts are not their gifts.

Key #3 Don't stay isolated

As I've mentioned before, one of Satan's greatest plans is to keep you isolated. When you are in the wilderness, it's hard to pull yourself out of bed in the mornings. I understand that depression can keep you from just wanting to walk to your kitchen, let alone walk to your bathroom to take a shower, get dressed, and then walk to your car to go somewhere. I won't forget what those days felt like. But I also won't forget that the biggest steps that I took forward were the times that my friends would force me to get out of my house. They would go to the store with me or take me to get our nails done together. Sometimes we just drove around and talked. Nausea and brain fog made it hard to function, and I felt like I was walking around in a shell; like I just wasn't really there. Changing up the routine and getting some fresh air always helped me, even if it was just a little. We sometimes make progress just one small step at a time, but any progress toward your freedom is better than none.

So much anxiety that was brought on by the pandemic directly resulted from Satan's plan to isolate. I've seen too many Christians just completely stop going to church because of fear. I'm trying so hard not to judge because I can only imagine how different the last few years would have been for me had God not freed me from the fear and anxiety.

Hebrews 10:24-25 says,

> *And let us consider one another in order to stir up love and good works, not forsaking the assembling of ourselves together, as is the manner of*

some, but exhorting one another, and so much the more as you see the Day approaching.

As we draw closer and closer to Christ's return, we are supposed to make gathering even more of a priority than ever before. The early church in the book of Acts gathered daily, yet here we are told to do it much more. I think it's extremely sad that we have trouble making it to church once a week. Perhaps our lack of gathering together more often is a major reason for the devastation we witness all over the world and the reason that so many are still living in bondage.

I believe God has placed a special calling on your life. If you're not careful, Satan will use isolation as a tool to keep you in chains, unable to move forward to become all that God has designed you to be. Why do you think you are fighting this fight? It's because Satan sees your potential and he's doing all that he can to hold you back.

Key #4   Seek out a trusted friend or mentor

This is something that I wish I had done when I was going through the thick of things. Unfortunately, when I was suffering, there was no one else with whom I could share what I was going through who would understand it… or so it seemed. Now I realize that I just didn't search hard enough. I guarantee there are people just like me who have overcome the great trials of fear, anxiety, and depression, who are right under your nose, but they just haven't shared their stories. Too many people keep their testimonies a secret because they're ashamed or think no one cares. Now that I'm on the other side of things, I see just how valuable my testimony is to others. I have a friend who is currently fighting anxiety. It helps her so much when I share with her what God has done for me. It gives her renewed hope that He will do the same for her. I send her Bible verses just about every single day and I'm always available for her phone calls and sometimes meet her to pray over her. All those things help bring peace to her anxious soul.

It would greatly benefit you to find someone who is on the other side of this journey who can be available to help you as you walk toward your freedom and deliverance. I would start at church by asking around. Ask your friends or the leaders if they know of anyone who has overcome what you are currently dealing with. People who have found victory are usually more than happy to share their story, pray with you, and walk alongside you.

Key #5   Increase your giving

I'm sure many people would want to just skip right over this section. Many people feel like they are struggling to make ends meet, so the last thing they want to hear is some lady telling them they need to increase their giving. Believe me, I understand; but stay with me for a minute. I'm sharing with you parts of my story that I know for a fact helped lead to my breakthrough, and when I increased my tithe from ten percent to eleven percent, there was an instant shift in my life.

Maybe you're not ready to give eleven percent or more. Perhaps you don't even tithe yet. If not, that's a great place to start. This is such an individual decision, so my advice is to pray and ask the Lord how He wants to use you with your time and your money, then sit back and listen for His answer. You may give plenty financially, but maybe God wants you to give more of your time serving others.

II Corinthians 9:6 says, "But this I say: He who sows sparingly will also reap sparingly, and he who sows bountifully will also reap bountifully." I truly believe that when you sow good seeds, God will bless you back in ways you could never even imagine. What if planting a seed in faith is the gateway to your breakthrough? Pray about it and then step out in faith and do what the Lord is calling you to do; give in whatever way He is leading you to give. I've not once regretted our giving when it was led by the Holy Spirit. There have been several times that God has stretched us to give in ways that seemed impossible, but He always came through and met every need that we faced.

Key #6   Speak godly declarations over your life

When I purposely wrote declarations in my journal and was faithful to speak them out loud, I often experienced supernatural breakthrough from the bondage that was holding me back. What battles are you currently facing? Write some declarations to say each day to help you combat the fight you're in. Be sure to include truths from scripture. For example, if you are struggling financially and that is a source of depression, write something like, "I am a child of the Most High King. My Daddy owns the cattle on a thousand hills. Because of Who my Father is, I shall lack no good thing." If it's fear that is tormenting you, you can write, "His perfect love has cast out ALL fear! Satan can no longer torment my mind because I have the mind of Christ. My mind is full of calm, peaceful thoughts."

I feel prompted by the Holy Spirit to speak directly to someone who may be battling a spirit of suicide. You know deep in your gut that it's the enemy's plan to take you out, but you're tired of fighting and trying to believe that tomorrow will be better than today. I speak to your spirit right now and call forth the warrior that is in you. By God's strength, you WILL make it! You will live and not die! You will find purpose and hope again. The battle is not yours, but His, says the Lord! I speak boldness over you to declare every day that the joy of the Lord is your strength. God loves you and He can use the hardest times of your life as a pathway to the best things that can ever happen to you. Don't give up!

Once you know what declarations you want to start speaking, it may be best to write them on a little note card and put them in places where you will be more likely to see them, like on your refrigerator. I have written some of mine on my bathroom mirror with a dry erase marker before. Figure out how you can keep them in front of you, so they won't just be written and forgotten about.

Key #7 Delegate things to other people

I don't know about you, but for me, a cluttered, disorganized home makes me restless. But as much as I would try to clean up my house, my efforts would usually fail. The Lord showed me it was because I was trying to do it all on my own. Sometimes I still struggle when my husband does the laundry. It just makes me feel like I'm not a good enough wife because he works all day, and he really shouldn't have to do laundry too. What am I getting at here? Well, as much as I wish he didn't have to help me with housework, the truth of the matter is that if he wants clean clothes, I might need his help sometimes. The same goes for giving our children chores. Since a cleaner home makes me feel less anxious, everyone who lives under this roof now pitches in to help. No more guilt because it's for my sanity, which affects everyone here!

I'm just using the clean home as an example because it's an area of my life where I've learned the benefits of delegating some work to others. Having a cleaner home helps my mind rest, and it allows me the time to do more of the things I enjoy.

Are you highly overwhelmed in a certain area of your life? If so, then maybe it's time to see where you can start giving more responsibility to others. Being too busy could be a source of anxiety and depression in your life and you may not even realize it. Delegating things to other people brings peace! In Exodus 18:13-27 when Moses was doing too much, his father-in-law told him it wasn't good because he would wear himself out. He told Moses to delegate all the smaller issues to other people to make it easier for him. In verse 23 (AMP) after Moses' father-in-law had told him to delegate to others, he says to him, "If you do this thing and God so commands you, then you will be able to endure [the responsibility], and all these people will also go [back] to their tents in peace."

Key # 8 Increase your prayer life

I have a feeling that most of the people reading this book have cried out to God many times asking Him to heal them in the areas where they feel broken. Whether that's you or not, continuing to ask the Lord for His help is never a bad thing. My mom always used to tell me I wasn't really trusting God if I kept asking Him over and over for His help with the same thing. I grew up believing what I'd been told all my life, but as I became an adult and buried myself in God's Word, I discovered that I had been lied to!

Luke 18:1-8 tells us a story about a persistent widow. Widows were often among the most vulnerable people, and apparently, this woman had no other family members to help plead her case. The wicked, unjust judge despised the woman and her cause and clearly considered her a nuisance. He finally broke down and gave her what she was asking for, not because he cared about her, but because she disturbed him with her persistent pleas. This story doesn't mean that we are badgering a reluctant God to meet our needs; but if an unjust judge will occasionally give us justice, how much more will the righteous, loving Judge of all the earth have mercy and grant us our heart's desires?

Here are a few more verses that prove that God wants us to remain prayerful about our circumstances:

> *So I say to you, ask and keep on asking, and it will be given to you; seek and keep on seeking, and you will find; knock and keep on knocking, and the door will be opened for you. Luke 11:9 (AMP)*

Rejoicing in hope, patient in tribulation, continuing steadfastly in prayer. Romans 12:12

Rejoice always, pray without ceasing. I Thessalonians 5:16-17

Key # 9   Schedule a doctor appointment

As I mentioned in chapter 4, sometimes your body can be all out of whack, and you can be totally unaware. If you haven't seen a doctor or had your blood work checked in a long time, then I would make that a priority. What if you are like me and just one tweak of a vitamin could be the thing you need to stop the heart palpitations and anxiety? You never know until you get it checked! Don't allow fear to stop you from seeing the doctor. This could be your ticket to freedom!

Key # 10   Study the Word

This is probably my favorite thing that helped me more than anything else. As I spent more time reading my Bible, praying for revelation, and searching for understanding, I could literally feel the old wineskin coming off as God clothed me with the new wineskin. See Mark 2:22 if you're confused by that reference. It wasn't an immediate difference, but as I continued to press into my daily commitment to the Word of God, I began experiencing less fear and anxiety. I also noticed that oppression was being lifted, and I found joy like I had never known before.

If you have trouble focusing on scripture reading, then I encourage you to search YouTube or download the Bible app and search for "The Bible Project." They have videos that walk you through scripture as they break it down for you in a way that you can understand. It was during my one-year Bible reading plan with The Bible Project that my freedom truly accelerated.

Key # 11   Revisit words that have been spoken over your life

Have you ever received a prophecy or a word from someone that gave you such hope for your future? What happened to it? Has it come to pass? Even if it's something that has already taken place in your life, are you sure you didn't miss any details? If you have access to a past word that once sparked new dreams and ambitions for your life, it may be time to bring it back to the surface and meditate on it once again. Whenever I do this, it gives me a new drive to focus harder on those promises that I know are mine.

Key # 12   Give your heart to God

I wrote this book understanding that most of the people who will read it are already saved. But what if you're not? Or what if you're not sure? No matter what you've grown up believing, no matter how old you are, and no matter what your past has looked like, GOD LOVES YOU! He longs for you to open your heart up to Him. It's as simple as believing in your heart that Jesus came and died for you. Salvation is not a list of dos and don'ts. It's a relationship with the Lord. It's a willingness to radically change your old ways of thinking and renew your mind as you focus your eyes on Christ. Don't think that you have to get yourself cleaned up before you give your life to Him. Jesus came for the broken and the lost, and tomorrow is promised to no one.

For it is by grace [God's remarkable compassion and favor drawing you to Christ] that you have been saved [actually delivered from judgment and given eternal life] through faith. And this [salvation] is not of yourselves [not through your own effort], but it is the [undeserved, gracious] gift of God; not as a result of [your] works [nor your attempts to keep the Law], so that no one will [be able to] boast or take credit in any way [for his salvation]. Ephesians 2:8-9 (AMP)

For God so loved the world that He gave His only begotten son, that whoever believes in Him should not perish but have everlasting life. John 3:16

I absolutely cannot imagine going through the darkest moments of my life without Christ. Sometimes I had no one else to talk to. As crazy as it may sound, when I poured my heart out to this God that no one can physically see, I just knew that He was right there with me, comforting me and bottling up my tears. And there have been too many events in my life like the tumor just disappearing, that no scientist or any other person on earth can explain. Putting my hope in Jesus gave me new strength that helped me endure the hard times and it gave me a greater expectation of great things for my future.

But those who wait on the LORD shall renew their strength; They shall mount up with wings like eagles, they shall run and not be weary, they shall walk and not faint. Isaiah 40:31

Key # 13   Choose to walk in faith.

Fear is typically something that you can see or sense, but faith is believing in the unseen and unknown.

Now faith is the substance of things hoped for, the evidence of things not seen. Hebrews 11:1

You've probably heard the saying faith over fear, but what exactly does that mean? How can you make the choice to walk in faith when you feel so bound by fear? It's honestly about taking a good look at your situation and understanding the potential danger but making the choice to fight through all your feelings and trust God anyway. With His help, you will drive out the fear and replace it with faith. You can do this! Take everything you've learned and give it all to God in prayer. Move forward with Him, trusting that He is right there with you, holding your hand as He promises in Isaiah 41:13.

Faith over fear usually requires action because you believe that what you need to do is worth the potential risks, just like when Peter stepped out of the boat to walk on water. Even though he had never walked on water before and it seemed impossible, he put his faith in the One who called him out. It wasn't until he took his eyes off Jesus that he began to sink. Faith requires us to keep our eyes on Jesus!

Final Note

~

God's Special Path Just for You

No matter what your past looks like, God can use your broken pieces to create a beautiful new life. Don't allow fear to hold you back from your full potential. One of my all-time favorite quotes is hanging up in our bathroom and serves as a constant reminder that even when we feel like we are too far gone, it's not too late for things to turn around in our favor. God is working in the background even when we don't feel like there's any action taking place. The quote says, "Just when the caterpillar thought the world was over, it became a butterfly." So, when you feel you've hit rock bottom, don't give up. It's at that place that you may discover your wings!

How do you figure out what God has called you to do?

First, realize that no one else can do it for you. There is no one else on this planet that has the same gifts and abilities as you do. What has God called YOU to do? Don't seek answers from other people. Instead of searching online, search your own heart. If you have a Bible, then you have the answers! If you would just get into the Word of God and ask Him for wisdom and guidance, He will show you. He will put you on a straight path.

Trust in the LORD with all your heart. Do not depend on your own understanding. In all your ways obey him. Then he will make your paths smooth and straight. Proverbs 3:5-6 (NIV)

As this book ends, I would love to prophesy into your life one last time. I pray these words will fall on open ears and an open heart.

God says that you are an overcomer and more than a conqueror. You have a sound mind that will no longer be shaken. I decree and declare right now that torment no longer has a hold on you. You will no longer allow the spirit of fear to press you down or hold you back. He who is in you is greater than he who is in the world. I speak to the root of all your fears and command it to be destroyed at once, taking down every other thing that was attached to it. The only seeds that have permission to take root in your life are the seeds that bear good fruit.

You will walk in complete freedom from fear, anxiety, panic, depression, and oppression in Jesus's name! I speak supernatural healing over every area of your life that the enemy has damaged. I prophesy a wall of protection over you that the enemy cannot penetrate. I pray God will even hide you from the enemy for a season as He builds you up in His strength. I speak the peace of God over you right now, flooding your soul until it overflows.

You are God's child. He loves you and fights for you. I pray for His presence to overtake you and I pray you will never forget His faithfulness. Your eyes will be opened to God's plans, and you will see that He has already equipped you with everything you need to move forward. You are not timid because His Word says that He gave you power. You will step into your calling with a Holy boldness, and you will be used to set the captives free! It is in Jesus's name I pray and decree these words over you. Amen!

God wants to take all that the enemy has tried to destroy you with and use it for His good to glorify His name. So, what is it? What tried to take you out? Where do all your fears stem from? Label it! But don't label it as a fear anymore. Give it to God and tell Him to show you how it can be used for His glory. Label it as victory! He's ready to do a major work in your life. He has given you the keys that you need and now He waits for your obedience. Do what He's leading you to do and watch the blessings flood into your life and those around you.

> *The LORD bless you and keep you; The LORD make His face shine upon you, and be gracious to you; The LORD lift up His countenance upon you, and give you peace. Numbers 6:24-26*

May your life forever be blessed by His peace!

My Final Reflections

ABOUT THE AUTHOR

Amanda Rosen is a Christian, homeschooling mom of four boys, originally from Ohio, but now resides in Lexington, KY. She is passionate about pulling people out of the darkness and leading them down a pathway to freedom. She has prayed for and counseled many people through their journeys to healing, using the tools that have freed her from a life of fear, anxiety, and depression. Her writing accomplishments include co-authoring the children's book, *Pushups and Crunches* with her husband, Aaron Rosen.

ACKNOWLEDGEMENTS

This book began as a seed that was planted in my heart over thirteen years ago. It was then that Prophet Ed Traut told me that I would use all the hurt and heartache that I had been through to write books that would help set people free. At the time he spoke those words, I didn't have any reason to believe him because I was still so bound by depression, fear, and anxiety. Yet every time I longed for a change in my life, I would go back over that prophecy and pray about what steps the Lord would have me take. Although I always loved writing, I didn't have the urge to write a book, and quite frankly, I didn't think I was good enough, or that anyone would care to listen to what I had to say.

But suddenly, about five years ago, the Lord told me that it was time. He put the words in my heart, and so I began typing them out. Within the last couple of years, God put an urgency in my spirit to finish what I had started. So, I thank Prophet Ed Traut for being God's faithful and obedient messenger. He has spoken into my life many times since that original prophecy and every word has been accurate and helpful.

I thank the Lord, Jesus Christ, for telling me that I am good enough and that this book will change people's lives. I thank Him for taking me from being a quitter, to becoming a woman who perseveres to the very end. I thank Him for the trials and hardships that I endured, for without the testing, there is no testimony. He has led me out of bondage and has given me a freedom that is almost indescribable. Without the Lord, I am nothing.

There are so many people who have contributed to this book. Some of them don't even know that they are a part of my story. I thank every person mentioned in the book, even those who caused pain because I know that God allowed it for a reason. I grew in the stretching and in the breaking, and I became aware of just how strong I really am.

I also give my thanks to the following people:

Aaron: You are my number one fan! You have learned how to encourage me in all the right ways. Thank you for loving me through the process of writing this book. Thank you for holding down the fort every time I needed the quiet time to write, and for your honest feedback as we worked together to make the necessary changes. Most of all, thank you for standing right by my side as I walked through the fear, anxiety, and depression. When no one else was there for me, you were! Even when you couldn't understand it, you still loved me and proved your love for me through your words and actions. I can't imagine life without you. I love you!

Gavin, Grisham, Garrison, and Gracen: So much of my story revolves around each of you; especially you Gavin, since you made me a mother twenty-three years ago. God hand-picked each of you just for me! You have given me extra joy, entertainment, laughter, and a reason to be proud. I love you, my sons, with all my heart!

Mom, you always believed in me, even when I didn't believe in myself. You were a shoulder to cry on when I wanted to give up. And on my darkest days, you spoke hope back into my life.

Dad, I'm thankful for the work God has done in your own life so that my own story could have a happy ending. Thank you for all of the sacrifices you have made over the years for our family.

My brothers: Where would a little sister be without her big brothers? I'm thankful for all of the times you protected me at home and at school. I know that you love me, and nothing will ever stand in the way of that.

Thank you to my grandmothers for always pointing me to Jesus.

Our family: Thank you to each one who has loved and supported me, even after we moved away.

My friends: I am so thankful for all of the friendships God has blessed me with, but there are a few that I just have to mention by name because they are the ones who have seen me at my absolute worst and loved me through it. Trish Richey, I sometimes feel like I don't deserve you. There were many years of my life when you were my only true friend. You made such an impact on me when you would come and drag me out of the house when I didn't want to get off the couch. You were always such a shining light to the darkness that surrounded me. Thank you for walking through the hard times with me! Melissa Sheehan, you are the sister that I longed for all my life. Thank you for sweeping me away to your cabin in the woods to work on this book, even though no writing was accomplished. God certainly used that time to bring us closer together and I am forever grateful. Cynthia Brewer, (aka Cindylou and my church momma); I'm thankful for all our taco dates where we have laughed, shared our hearts, and wiped our faces because of our leaking eyes. You have spoken such wisdom into my life and helped me to always stand on what God's Word says, no matter what my circumstances look like.

Pastors Brent and Colleen Ireland, you both saw whom God called me to be, well before I could see it for myself. Thank you for speaking it into existence!

Pastor Chuck Balsamo, thank you for your encouragement and for your suggestions on my book title! You are such an inspiration to me.

Last, but certainly not least, I thank my wonderful editor, Lisa Vest. Lisa, you have been absolutely amazing to work with! You have been such a gift from God through this entire process. What I love the most about you is that you listened to me and allowed this book to be exactly what I believe the Lord wanted it to be. Thank you!

www.ingramcontent.com/pod-product-compliance
Lightning Source LLC
Chambersburg PA
CBHW041144110526
44590CB00027B/4115